After the Violence

An Intimate Portrayal of Life After Abuse

By Sophia Grace

ISBN 978-1-5406-9064-7

ISBN13 1540690644

Printed in the United States of America

Dedicated to all the men and women who have dared to
dream of a life AFTER THE VIOLENCE
and to those who have dedicated their lives to
shelter & support each of us along our way.

"In the United States, an average of 20 people are physically abused by intimate partners every minute.
This equates to more than 10 million victims annually."[1]

If you need help, call the National
Domestic Violence Hotline at 1-800-799-SAFE (7233)
or go online to DomesticShelters.org.

---

[1] NCADV. (2015). *Domestic violence national statistics.* Retrieved from www.ncadv.org.

AUTHOR'S NOTE

My story is kind to those who do not know me. My life has been blessed by four wonderful daughters: Ashley, Rebecca, Christy, and Elsie. In some ways, I have a perfect life. My days are filled with their laughter. My mind is challenged by their insights. It is another story for those who have walked these years with me.

My family was torn at the hands of abuse. I have survived cancer, multiple surgeries, and loss of friendships. My children have each had to choose between suicide and moving on with their lives.

At points, my daughters and I have debated if autobiographies are fact or fiction. After all, the stories we tell ourselves are embedded with errors and warped by our perspective and judgments. While this story is inspired by my family's life and healing, it is in no way an act of non-fiction. Many of the names have been changed. The conversations have been recreated. Locations have been omitted.

The true power of my story is not in the legalistic details, but how it can plead with you, the reader, to enter the emotional and confusing mess of leaving domestic violence. As an autistic, single mother, my interpretation of life can bring a bit of levity to an otherwise overwhelming and painful topic.

As is always the case, there are many conflicting memories and opinions of these events. I am certain each of us will inevitably write history to favor ourselves. I did not write this book to cause anyone harm. My only desire has been to let others see my struggles with domestic violence, intimacy, parenting, and spirituality through my eyes.

#1. TYING THE KNOT

I made a mistake early on: I married a man I did not love and could not fully trust. On the surface, there was no reason for my doubts or concerns. He was kind, a good listener, and protective. We had met at a church event. We volunteered together taking food to low-income families each week. To the outsider, he was wonderful. He had worked as a security guard in the hospital, as a campus pastor, and as a counselor for the addicted. A year after we met, he asked me out.

It may sound strange that I did not love a man who seemed "perfect," but no matter how hard I tried to deny it, I could sense danger. I felt like a fish being bumped by a shark; nothing had happened, but I knew I was not safe.

Looking back at my journals, I see the signs more clearly. My entries are filled with comments like, "I feel trapped by Frank's momentum." "He's so sure it is God's will that he won't even give me time to think." "After I am with him, I feel physically sick, emotionally-pressed, and spiritually torn."

He didn't press me for sex during our engagement, but soon after we married, he made it clear that I was his possession and had better enjoy sex at a moment's notice. He came on very strongly. He was romantic and cunning. The things I thought showed kindness and humility turned out to be fronts to safeguard his image. He was a narcissist addicted to sex.

People at church encouraged me to dismiss my fears before we married. I remember comments like, "If anyone listened only to fear, no one would get married," "You can't back out now; it would just be selfish and rejecting," and "All men just want to have sex, stop being so tied up in yourself and marry him." They encouraged me to follow my fiancé's lead since our relationship was "from God." But in my heart, I questioned, "How am I supposed to feel safe in a controlling relationship? How can I submit to his protection when I constantly feel on my guard with him?"

Despite feeling as though I had been tossed out to sea with a predator looming nearby, I married Frank in a small country church before my friends and family. The first few weeks went smoothly. He was content as long as he had all my attention. But as life wore on, it became apparent that I really was in danger.

#2. REALITY SINKS IN

The physical abuse began a few months after the wedding. Frank was controlling with finances. He isolated me from people I knew. He drained every drop of vitality from my soul, but he had not yet hit me.

That changed when he found out I was pregnant. Jealous that our child could demand attention by making me throw up, he became psychotically jealous. He took on the task of controlling all my attention and affection with physical violence.

He beat me for being distracted when he spoke to me. He hit me for scratching dry skin on my calves, after a shower, because it meant I was not looking at him. In all honesty, it didn't matter what the excuse was. He delighted in controlling my body as if I were a puppet that he could move as he desired.

Soon, he looked at physical violence as the way to create his perfect life: sex whenever he wanted. He wanted to ensure that he was respected as a god.

On a little piece of scrap paper, I wrote: "He is beating me multiple times per day. He says he is doing it because I am a bad wife. I don't even know how to be a good wife. He tells me that I am controlling and stubborn, that I need to be punished. I think he just does it because he is addicted to sex. He has a whole ritual to it: 1) tell me how I have transgressed, 2) beat me until I have no fight left and beg for his forgiveness, 3) force me to have sex." He wasn't out-of-control or drunk when he was violent. He was methodical. Often, he would pray for me as he beat me.

I have heard people talk about the cycle of abuse. Supposedly, abusers will go through periods of remorse and apologize, followed by a period of kindness, only to end with another episode of physical violence. Frank was not like that. He never apologized. Those first few years, there were no periods of remorse or manipulative thoughtfulness.

His abuse had a different cycle. If, after he had beaten me, I was not instantly ready for sex, he would justify hitting me more. I was struck simply for making his shoulder sore after he had already spanked me with a toilet plunger for hours. He would beat me for not smiling at him instantly whenever I saw him. He would beat me for spending 20 cents over in an area of our budget. Honestly, he just made up reasons.

I regularly had bruises, welts, and broken skin under my clothes. During the first year of our marriage, Frank performed his "ritual" literally hundreds of times.

He used an answering machine with a feature like a baby monitor to make sure I was home during the day. He became paranoid that I was cheating on him. If he called and I was not able to answer, I would be beaten when he got home.

I quickly learned, as any sex slave does, that offering sex first could sometimes short circuit his pattern. As my pregnant stomach got bigger, Frank began to fear that I would gain too much weight and would no longer meet his needs. It was at that point that he went as far as beating me if I ate before HE heard my stomach growl. It was as if, when we married, Frank lost any sense that I was a separate person with a separate body. I was his, to do with as he pleased.

I had to be ready at any time, day or night, to satisfy his addiction. He would beat me simply for not being ready for sex, or being too dry for him, on a moment's notice. My entire appearance had to be centered around him. I was beaten for not wearing lipstick when he came home from work. For not standing when he walked in the room (even when I was multiple months pregnant, and it was hard to get up). He beat me for over an hour for picking up a box, justifying the punishment because the strain of lifting the box could harm the baby or me. In his mind, hitting me for hours with a stick and praying for me and shoved fingers in my vagina as part of the punishment, made more sense.

As the years went by, he could get me to do what he wanted with just a threatening glance. I have heard people say that God works all things for good. I have often pondered what good could have come from my experience. As I had more children, I learned the art of trying to redirect his attention to me, being a lightning rod of sorts for his anger and desires.

I have not found any good come from those experiences that could not have been discovered in other ways. There is only one thing that I am grateful for during that time; God did not abandon me. In the depths of pain, when the beatings seemed to go on forever, when the hours had passed and yet he continued, Frank forced me inside of myself, into my depths, where I rode my breath from one side to another. He pushed me to the point that I could almost touch God, like a baby pressing against its mother, through the walls of the womb.

#3. THREADING THE NEEDLE

It was in those moments—
As he prayed for me for being a bad wife,
As he spanked me with the toilet plunger, a belt,
Whatever he could find,
As he waited until I submitted with slow, methodical breaths,
And then raped me again—
That I remembered
Your tender embrace,
The glint in Your eyes,
The controlled power and restraint
You held my hands as I followed You across creeks,
Stepping from rock to rock
You guarded and protected my every step,
Scared that I might get hurt
And yet, here
He was
Beating me
Welts and bruises. Cut skin. Dislocations
I could not love enough

He served one purpose
Himself
His message in conflict
With me—
I didn't need to be changed
He did

I feel as though I grabbed on to You
And even though I couldn't
See You
I held so tightly that I pulled You back
Through my body

Looking at the poem now, I see it differently. Just as I had held so tightly onto God, I have begun to see how He also has held on to me. He has used His body, all the other people He created, to pull me back from the brink of despair. He still has a hold of me. Being near God has not always been an easy thing, and I am sure that there are many better ways to do it.

Frank's abuse provoked anger as well. It unleashed an unparalleled passion toward God, both good and bad. It made me question who God even is and why He allows these things to occur. I explored these issues with Him in poetry. The irony, of being prayed for and beaten at the same time, warped my ability to trust others while they prayed, even people I had known for years. We tried marriage counseling. He went to domestic violence treatment. He attended a group for sex offenders, but the abuse continued.

#4. ASKING WHY

Okay, God, I'm here
Trying to figure this out
What the FUCK is wrong
With YOU
And Your people?
In what insane universe

Did You think?!?
That this life
Was okay?
You're screwed

If it is true
That the church is Your wife
You better, God, believe
That the part I am going to play first
Is to tell You a thing or two
about how stupidly
You screwed this up
You are insane
You're a jerk, and even as
Passionately as I love You
I'm through!

#5. SWEARING

I have been told that God forbids swearing and that I should not say "fuck" in a prayer. To which I reply, if you had to run a red light anywhere in the heart of the city, which intersection would you choose? Me? I'd run the red light right in front of the police station. Officers are trained to watch for people doing stupid things and the public is more careful near police stations. While I might get a ticket, I'd have the least possibility of losing my life or killing someone else. People are cautious in prayer, even though God hears every word and emotion they have. I'd rather be real than try to design my speech, deadening out the pain, to make it palatable for God.

#6. BABY FACTORY

As only rape and sex multiple times a day can do, I got pregnant over and over. After only a few years, I was balancing Frank's incessant need for attention and sex, all the while, caring for four young children. When my youngest was born, the others were ages four, three, and two. Any mom would have been exhausted, but I had a deeper concern. I feared my inability to keep his abuse directed at me and away from my children.

The insanity of his excuses to beat me made me doubt if I wasn't just trapped in an atrocious dream. Everyone else seemed to view him as a sensitive, compassionate saint, except for my mother who always knew there was something askew.

I remember at the time trying to wake up and snap out of it. I would argue with myself, "Frank beats me for eating or not eating as if it is a diet program to ensure I don't gain too much weight to please him. How can a mind make sense of that? It's crazy. It's psychotic. But it is making it so hard for me to figure things out. Everyone seems to think he is such a great husband. After all, he has a devoted wife and four obedient kids."

But in my secret journal, the pages held sentences that were closer to my heart. "Please keep me safe today or be with me when I am not." I didn't have time to write much more.

Or another day's entry, "God, I don't know how to keep the desire even to have my heart beat. Somehow, find the strength in me."

At various points in my pregnancies, I ended up on bedrest, locked in my home with my abuser, trying to figure out how to parent young children and rest.

My heart cried out, "How the hell am I supposed to parent without getting up? I need ideas like a dog throwing his ball down the stairs to stay active."

Ashley, my oldest, was still a toddler, but she could run circles around me even when I could stand. But more importantly, I begged God to teach me. I pleaded, "How am I supposed to keep Frank's attention, protect this baby, and protect Ashley?" My attention was divided and that no longer felt safe.

#7. SCARED

> I'm exhausted
> And anxious
> Scared
> I will not be able
> To meet the needs
> Of my kids
> Because
> I am fighting
> Exhaustion
> All the time

#8. NEEDING HELP

I felt like a burden on God since I was constantly throwing up prayers like a person with the stomach flu. Each one filled with my hesitancy, insecurity, and anger. My emotions were half-digested. I had to believe that God, like any good parent, could stand being covered in filth. My motto at the time: just keep talking.

> Okay, I'm sorry
> I know I should not
> be a bother
> I know I don't
> Make sense
> I probably should not
> Even speak
> But, really?
> What type of crazy god
> would let
> People
> Whose sole motivation is controlling
> And using other people?
> Be given residency
> On Earth?
> Abuse sucks
> And so does Your judgment

#9. HOW AM I DOING

When I separated from Frank, people inquired how I was doing, but I knew it was not yet safe to reply. It was only a greeting I found; very few people even wait for an answer. If silent, they didn't even question the lack of response. It was freeing, to be honest. Saying "Fine" or "Good" just didn't work. I was sad, confused, and angry. How was I really doing? I could only say that to God.

#10. THE ANGRY CRY OF PAIN

You suck
Not really, but I am FRUSTRATED
With You right now.
Remember when You rocked me
As I dissociated
From being beaten? It calmed me

Try and rock me now, if You dare
I doubt You can calm me
Down
Now, my kids and I are still here
Still just trying to get
Our footing

Everywhere I go reminds me of him
Go to the store, where he stalked me
Drive down the street and see
Where he pulled off to hit me
For talking back. Well
I'm TALKING back to You
NOW, pull over and just try
To hit me. Sorry, but I am desperate
I must have
Your attention
I need You to listen to me

I need You to meet

My basic needs and keep us

Safe

So he doesn't kill us

There it is. The truth

I need You to keep my kids and me

Alive

Forget the rest

Alive, please

That is my prayer

That's all. Goodnight

Oh, but I do want

To be the part

Of the bride

In Heaven

To tell You off

By that point

You should be able

To hear a smile behind my words

I could not find a way to say that in a conversation with people. How was I doing, in one word? Carwreck, but even that was two words.

#11. APPLYING FOR FOOD STAMPS

Getting out of the violence was not easy. There were challenges simply because of Frank's connections in our community.

I remember applying for food stamps

The first time

Crossing the rule of my husband

Sheltered

At the bottom of the form

Was a question

Is there anyone making you feel unsafe, hurting you?

I left it

Blank

Applying for aid

Could

Make him look bad

And I knew

He would punish me

Just for completing

The rest of the form

But

I handed it in

To the clerk at the desk

Did I finish

Each question, each line?

All but one

Before I could answer

He looked up

"Hey, aren't you married to Frank?"

Please, please

Don't say anything

Just mark no
I'm not here
Please don't share that I was...
Needing
HELP

#12. SAFEGUARDS

So many ways
To help people these days
Questions
Inserted as if
They provide
Safety

#13. WIC OFFICE

The WIC office was housed in the same building where Frank worked. Ideally, WIC (Women, Infants, and Children) ensures that pregnant women, new moms, and children obtain the nutrition and services they need, but sometimes people get overlooked.

In the same building WIC and Frank
Provided service
Counsel
Vouchers for food
Weight checks for babies
A safe place

But as I went in
To be questioned
My interviewer
A woman
Knew Frank
But apparently, the computer did not
"Is anyone abusive at home?"
Technology prompted

She glossed over the question
Marking "NO" the response
Before I could reply
Apologizing for intruding
And instead said,
"Sorry, it's awkward"

She stumbled
Explaining the truth
"We are supposed to ask
Everyone"
But frankly
She was too smart

At the end of the
Interview
I managed to say
Please don't skip that
Question

The answer is hidden
Deep in the walls
Of each home

What was it like to be married to Frank? In every way, the cost of being in public was to make him look good. Keeping truth silent. It was a smart ploy. If I ever did speak, I would be labeled crazy, since I would be contradicting even myself.

#14. THE PEDIATRICIAN

Of all the helpers
The doctor is surely the one
Most responsible
For the health and welfare
Of the children

During the appointment
My mind I yell out
He's throwing her
Against the wall at night
Hitting her head
And
Her headaches
They keep her in that bed

But I look at the doctor
And heard her comment
You have such a sweet

Husband
I see him at the library
He is so good with the kids

How do I follow that?

Could I just have
Postpartum psychosis
And just
Imagined it?
Because his image
Defies reality
He is so good
With them

But that is him
In public
Not
Getting a child
Into bed
The whole thing
Makes my head
Hurt, too

#15. THE ONE TO BLAME

We went to marriage counseling today. I told the pastor that my husband is still abusing me. The counselor replied, "Are you sure? Some people get in a rut and think everything is abuse. They exaggerate for attention."

I told him that I was aware of that pitfall. Being forced to justify my comment, I explained, "I had a fever of over 104 degrees this week with Strep throat. He crawled on top of me and rubbed his penis on me because he said the warmth got him off. It was one time he didn't have to beat me to make my skin hot. Do you think that is abusive enough for you?"

He turned to my husband, "You did that?"

"She was hot." These people are sick.

#16. NEEDING SILENCE

God, I read a book today and came to a conclusion. Every good story begins with a period. It's only when someone stops talking that there is truly time to reflect. Plus, and I know it is just my quirky understanding of language, but

> Women are magnificent
> Storytellers
> When we decide to
> Let go of what we cannot fix
> By nurturing
> When we choose to
> Let go
> And have a period
> Of rest
> I think God made us that way
> On purpose.

> But sometimes, I forget.

#17. THE WEAVING

Looking at my life as a tapestry not cut from the loom has helped me find rest while still working. It has helped me focus on the small task at hand and not the insurmountable challenges that lie ahead.

> Over, under, over
> Under, over, under
> I breathe
> In and out, in and out
> Calm
> I try again
> In, pause, pause, pause
> Out, pause, pause, pause
> Slowly reigning in
> My stress response

#18. DEFEAT

> It would have been
> Easy to give up
> To resign myself
> To never be heard

#19. PLEADING FOR REST

As I came to grips with the thousands of diapers I would change those first few years, I struggled. I had to find the centeredness I would need to get free. I had to somehow face, and reconcile, the discrepancy of life at home with Frank and the perception of him in the community.

"I need a break from trying to figure out my life. I am too tired to go on. I don't know if I can do this. Even if it is in the form of a tear, help me learn how to be in the eye of the storm, at least until that day when I have strength not to be."

#20. TAPESTRY OF MOONLIGHT

There were storytellers
In days of old, that spun tales of
Great power
And with sound they'd mold
The heart of a child
As they freed
Truth, far greater
That could never be sold

They captured minds
And lives
As they sought
To share a new story
A complicated plot
With wisdom foretelling
The power to change
Oh, where did they go?
Those minstrels so bold
Can they rewrite my story
Now that it's told?

My thread's all used up
My story half done
But despite even that
My warp is still snug
It lacks their hand
To finish the fight
And tell my story
A powerful plight

So, God, if they are ever
In search of a loom
Desired for weaving
Oh, let it be soon
Remember this site
My children and I
That they might weave
Our life's story
Into the sky

When I was younger my father made me a loom in his workshop. I have kept it through the years, but I have never finished a single blanket or rug. Instead I have looked at it and pondered my life. I have a dream that someday people, whom I have impacted with my life, will bring strings or scraps of material that they will then weave onto my loom.

#21. CONTRAST

As time elapsed, I came back to those times able to see the contrast between God and Frank. Instead of just blaming God that it happened or
questioning why, I began to see God as distinct, from Frank, and safe. It's
a theme I explored when I wrote about the reality of being abused.

> The truth, my experience here
> He beats me for wearing the wrong lipstick.
> You bring life and wonder to my lips.
> He beats me for not standing when he walks in the room.
> You fill the space around me no matter what position I am in.
> He beats me for carrying a box while pregnant.
> You carry me through that sin.
> He makes up reasons to beat me.
> Oh, what is wrong with him?

#22. LOOKING GOOD

Frank gave me money to buy clothes for the kids and then bragged to his
friends about how generous he was. He got what he wanted: accolades and
attention; all the while beating me if I went slightly over the $10 personal
toiletries and clothing budget. A few cents could warrant a punishment and
rape. It kind of felt like Frank gave me the money as an insurance policy
for his ego. No one would believe that he beat me over loose change when
he was so generous and kind.

I was exhausted. Even the smallest tasks that would have normally been easy to complete, got put on the back burner while I tried to come to grips with my life.

There were baskets in the bathroom with the tags still on them. I wanted to take them off, but I was too tired at the end of the days. Frequently, I fell asleep on my bed in the clothes I had worn that day. After all the chaos that comes with small children, I rarely had energy reserved to take care of me.

#23. SELF-CARE

One of my friends gave me a pedometer and said that exercise would make me feel better. Taking time for myself would help me as a mom. I got over 10k steps a day without ever leaving the 875-sq. ft. house. Honestly, I needed a nap more than exercise and would have been better served by babysitting than a pedometer, but the sentiment was sweet.

It seemed like people often gave solutions that would work in a "regular" house, not knowing how domestic violence changes things. I was bound not just by Frank's abuse and my exhaustion, but by the misconceptions other people had about abuse.

There is a double standard for women escaping violence. When a football player has a concussion, he is not shamed for being too confused to leave the game. The referees and coaches are expected to make the decision. In contrast, when a woman is abused, it is her fault if she does not leave. It is her fault if she stays and the abuse continues.

I tried to write, wondering if I could put the words onto paper that they might somehow make sense. With Frank's pattern of abuse, controlled and hidden, I ran into almost the opposite judgement. I "should" stay and support my husband. He was a productive, kind member of society. He was clearly devoted to his family. I was judged for wanting to get out. Later, I would be judged for how long I stayed.

And yet, there was a payoff for me that he felt he had to look good in public. I was glad that he had to keep up the image of the good husband; otherwise, there would have been no reprieve.

I don't understand why people can't see that domestic violence is not just in homes filled with poverty and drugs or homes in which people drink and have no emotional control. Violence in my home was purposeful and controlled. It was birthed by Frank's desire to control every aspect of my life, all the while keeping me dependent on him financially and emotionally.

#24. THE NARRATIONS OF LIFE

When most people
Look at a page
In a book
They see letters
In lines
Stacked in an effort
To encode one's
Feelings
Perceptions
And lies
But I
I
Just see
White

White shapes
Cut out of
Each page
With textures
And patterns
A snowflake
Of sorts
No reason
Nor rhyme

What is left
From the page
That was
Butchered
By time
My story is not
A freedom
It's a feeble attempt
To create
My blizzard

Most people think of storms as big, violent rains with winds and instability, but my storm was nearly silent. It came as a single tear. I wasn't running around. In fact, it didn't involve anyone other than my children and me.

Let me state it this way: when a child is young and crying out for food, a mother will give all she has to her infant. However, when the mother has nursed her baby until her body is parched, yet knows they will still die, she has a decision to make. Does she use her last drop of life to try and meet the need of her child, knowing full well that it is not enough? Or does she spill her last drop to honor her grief, filled with all the anger, bitterness, and flattened dreams, knowing full well that it will not guarantee her child will live? I contend that it is that drop of water that contains the full power of the storm.

#25. A DROP

A drop of blood is all it takes to infect someone with disease
A drop of sperm is all it takes to create a miniature me
But a teardrop, what is its power
Compared to the entire sea?

The chronic stress from abuse is disorienting. It drains every bit of energy from your life. The headaches, aching joints, and emotional trauma would leave anyone a mess. People should stop judging victims by silently (or vocally) criticizing each of our decisions. I wish, when people work with abuse survivors and victims, that they would treat those people with the kindness of a war-torn combat veteran who just returned from an awful deployment.

#26. WEAKNESS

Throughout my life, I have battled with muscle weakness. It is a neurological condition that, when left untreated, paralyzed attempts to defend myself. During those first few years of my marriage, I only had insurance when I was pregnant, but pregnancy left me unable to take the medication.

When police asked if I had ever screamed "No" or tried to push him off, all I could say was "No." My mouth went slack and my arms went weak in situations of extreme fear. They did it when I heard a joke, too, but my life had not been filled with humor since I married.

People don't realize the long-term ramifications of not providing health care to the poor. The issue is much more complicated than not wanting to enable people to live off the system. Sometimes, not covering insurance or medications can cause a multitude of problems, many more expensive than doctors' appointments and prescriptions.

#27. MISUNDERSTOOD

When Ashley was little
She screamed
Walking
To the bathroom
As I held two of her sisters
Incessant that
I hold her

Protesting
She demanded
My effort
But I couldn't
Given the other
Demands on my
Body
We made it
To the bathroom

Only to find
Sores from loose stools

My heart
Pinned down
She was being
Needy
Not in an attempt
To force me to
Hold her

She was at
God's mercy
And just
Exclaiming
Pain

I know women who have escaped from abuse can seem loud and annoying, pressing with needs. But maybe, it is that behavior that helped them finally escape. Maybe they are being hurt by things that no one can see. They could be irrational and annoying because something is causing them pain. Before you judge the incessant demands, pause and consider what they are walking in. Sometimes dirty diapers do more than just stink.

Some people might just want sympathy or delight in being needy. But the truth of abuse, it causes physical problems, not just emotional and mental ones.

#28. INTERVENTION

The most effective intervention I ever experienced was a simple question from a church elder's wife. She calmly said, "At some point, you need to ask yourself: do I truly feel safe with him?" That was it. She didn't give me a four-point lecture on the dynamics of abuse or tell me that he would do it again. She didn't try to scare me into leaving or promise that things could be better if I stayed or divorced. She just asked me to consider listening to my heart.

The strength of her response came from not trying to control mine. Instead, she helped me find that quiet voice in my heart. She helped me trust my intuition, knowing that when a woman listens to her intuition, she will have the best chance of survival for both herself and those in her care. The same is true for a man.

What followed was a series of challenges as I learned to hear my heart again and face some of the traumas that happened, not only by Frank's hands, but by the very people who were supposed to be there to help that didn't. There were also individuals who helped, ones who might never know their full impact.

I journaled, "Some grandmas came and helped me take care of my girls today. I'm on bedrest. Not sure how much is from stress and how much is abuse. But they came, brought peanut butter and jelly with smiley face napkins. It's good to have smiles in these walls."

Other times I wrote poems. Occasionally, I wrote them as if I was talking to people directly. One of my first was a poem about going to the OB/GYN appointments during my pregnancies.

Most of the things I wrote I just filed away in an old shoe box. However, this is one I sent in hopes that they'd be more careful.

#29. THE ILLUSION

My husband
He comes to all the appointments
"What a supportive partner you have," you say
But in reality he is a spy
You see he's been beating me. Raping me.

The bruise
I cover, I hide
I turn my body, so you don't see
But you see one that slips through
"How did you do that? Did you run into something?
"Yes."
I go home to get beaten for letting it show

Bedrest
I start having contractions
"You'll have to stop having sex," you say
"What? We can't."
You laugh
"Well, you need to," you reply, "sex can cause the baby to come
Early."

I Go Home
To cry
Sex can keep me from being beaten
And I can't stop it when he... oh, please don't hurt the baby

We're having sex three to five times a day

I call
You cancel my appointments while I am on bedrest
"Sounds like you're doing fine."
"But I don't like being home for so long."
"It sounds like you are doing fine."
I need your support
"It's only a few more weeks."
You don't get it; he doesn't beat me before my appointments.
I desperately long to hear if the baby is okay

Antidepressants
I try to tell you; I burst into tears
"I cry all the time," I weep
"A lot of pregnant women do that," you say
My husband uses the bathroom
"But it's just hard. I..." I stammer for words.
You give me a prescription for an antidepressant and the time
Ends.
15 minutes sharp

The exam
I'm shaky and scared
"I feel anxious lying here."
"Everyone does. I'll make it quick."
But it reminds me of being raped
Soon everything goes numb.
Measurements, heartbeat

Look at my face, my spirit pleads
Don't you see the pain?

After the birth
Part of the placenta is left attached
You go in, ready to scrape.
I scream
The medication makes me slightly dissociated
For hours, I relive the rapes
I thought you were safe
I thought it was only him

Checking out
"Are you safe at home?" the nurse asks
My husband dutifully stands by

I wish that more people "got it." That pastors and doctors were sensitive to the effects of violence. I wish more men and politicians were talking about domestic violence. There are plenty of people affected.

The demands of caring for young children provided a distraction from the sirens of alarm in my spirit for safety. The annoyances of my kids offered relief.

I found a scrap of paper on which I wrote, "Ashley made life interesting today. She took off Becca's diaper in the car and smeared poop all over everything. Becca's face, the windows, the seats were covered. What was I doing? I dared take a minute to say goodbye to a friend. In less than two minutes, she decided to become an artist." That was the amount of time it took for Ashley to quadruple the amount of work I had when I got home.

#30. DISAPPOINTMENT

Today I feel
Like a little kid
Staring out
On a rainy day
Watching
My sandbox
Become
Mud

I am watching
My life
Be torn apart
Wrestling just
To keep it
Bound
Together

The events
With my kids
Are normal
Yet special
But no matter
How funny
They play

Frank's violence

Devours

Their laughter

It is something

That's looming

Ruining the day

#31. IMPENDING ISOLATION

During my marriage, Frank made it clear that I was not allowed to spend time with people without him and that there would be consequences if I talked. As we separated, the isolation became even more intense. I could be apart from him, but he would be there, keeping an eye on me and making sure I obeyed. He followed me to the grocery store. He moved into the neighbor's house across the street under the pretense of just needing quiet and that being impossible with four kids at home. He kept his eye on us like an eagle watches fish.

He checked with my old friends to see what I had shared. The level of isolation he imposed was deafening. That said, there was one group of people he did not have the power to control.

Our house sat halfway between the closest bus stop and foreign student housing for the university. Every hour and five minutes, we would have international students walking down our street. During the day, when Frank was at work, I would go out and invite people in. Unconventional, yes, but it worked. Most of the students, or more often their wives, would come in and be grateful for some hot tea and a chance to converse. When I would tell the women that they were welcome anytime during the day, but after four could not come over because my husband would be home, they nodded with understanding. Many of them had children who would come over, too. My kids loved playing with those children, but they knew not to talk about it when Frank came home.

I learned something interesting from those women, even when we struggled to converse. I learned that people could speak with only their presence. They taught me how to sit with God.

#32. ONE NIGHT A WEEK

One of the ways that I tried to ensure safety was to rent out one of the rooms of our home one evening a week. Those nights Frank usually did not come home. He was grateful for the supplemented income for the room; although, I have often wondered if he was also thankful for the night to indulge his sexual obsessions.

Those were the nights that I wrestled with God over divorce. He showed me that real intelligence has the wisdom to know when to break the rules and scripts I had been taught. Any computer can follow code, but knowing when not to follow it, that is a sign of true intelligence and creativity. Sure, we all should follow laws, tell the truth, and obey the speed limit, but there are points when you need to follow the spirit of the law, more than the law itself. This deduction holds its full significance in families filled with violence. Sure, marriage is a covenant for life. Yes, children should listen and obey their parents. But when there is violence, when there is terror, divorce and separation prove God's standard of love more than staying.

I am certain, if you keep reading, I will offend you at some point. Just skip those parts, but the part about divorce honoring God's standard of love I will not go back on. I will warn you, though, be careful at what you throw out. Sometimes the truth can be offensive simply by being itself.

#33. CHILD WELFARE

Child welfare called today. They got a report that Christy cut her hair. The woman was confused; she had to investigate, but she also apologized for having to look into it.

Apparently, she had taken Ashley out of class at school to question her. How did Christy get the scissors? Where were they? What was I doing at the time? Where was I when it happened?

"Your mom was in the other room, reading with Rebecca? The scissors were in the kitchen drawer. You got them and gave them to your sister? Did Christy cut herself or something? No, just her hair. Huh?"

Another child welfare investigation, solved. Sure, they could dismiss all reports of Frank abusing the girls since they knew him personally and he testified in some of their cases. If they were with me even a bad haircut was worth investigating. Heck, Ashley throwing applesauce on the ceiling warranted a visit.

I continued, "God, I know they need to do their jobs, but this is ridiculous. Cut hair? Applesauce? I wonder if these would even be considered if they weren't best buds with Frank. He can manipulate so many people! It's frustrating."

However, feeling targeted has never helped anyone. All I could do was keep steady. Keep doing what I could to protect the girls as much as I could. My best guess is they probably just saw the signs of abuse and misplaced them onto me. Regardless, their investigations never revealed neglect.

Of course, if they counted toddlers doing the dishes out front in the wading pool as neglect, it would have been another story. I was pulling out every stop trying to keep things working in our home at that point.

Maybe they were just accustomed to parents using drugs. Maybe some people had kids who never threw food at the ceiling or cut their hair. But my journal revealed how I felt, "Fuck it. The truth is: I am sick of trying to come up with reasons for why child welfare and my kids are acting the way they are. I don't do drugs. I have never smoked pot. I don't even take pain meds after surgery. Only once did I drink three glasses of wine, and that was at a wedding, which proved to me it was not worth repeating, so get over it. Parents like me do exist. We might be rare, but we exist, and we need to be taken as we are."

I felt conflicted, feeling like I had to defend myself with child welfare and face the reality that I was fighting for my life to get us free from Frank. I read a quote years ago that stated "There is a certain freedom that comes with poverty... a freedom to be in utter despair." There is a freedom that comes from pain, too.

#34. THE QUILT

I remember sitting on the couch, holding my little girl. There were Cheerios all over the floor, the couch. I was exhausted, alone, and didn't know to whom I could turn.

I would say that I wrote down my prayer, but the truth was:

I had no prayer. I was in too much pain to speak, so I just sat.

I remember, at some point, looking around me as if every part of my surrounding had been a green screen, unimportant when contrasted to the abuse.

But behind me hung a quilt. One that had been made by a group of women who sat around at church and conversed as they made blankets to give to families with newborns. As I sat there, I started to think about the ladies who made that quilt and the time and effort they put into it. That blanket had been there with my daughters and I through it all.

Those ladies had supported me. They cared. They had the foresight to see me sitting there, alone and scared, holding my baby. As I sat under the shadow of that blanket, I meditated on all the pieces of fabric that it contained and tried to imagine all the people in the factories that wove the material, all the people who designed the patterns, and all the people who serviced the looms. I thought about the people who created the dyes that colored the threads. They had all given their time and lives to share their gifts with me. They were with me. I invited them to sit with me as I held my baby girl. I gave thanks that they had walked before me and prepared my home for that very moment.

After that, I started to think about all the things in my home: the silverware, the furniture, and the bricks around the fireplace. With each item, I imagined its creators coming into my little home and sitting with me in silence, with my pain, as I held my child. They filled my home, witnesses of violence.

I envisioned a network of support, as they came and sat with me through their gifts. They were with me. It no longer mattered that my parents had moved to another state or that I was being ostracized at church. It didn't matter that people questioned me, asking if I felt guilty for not trying harder to keep my marriage intact or that child welfare investigated want-to-be hairdressers and food throwers. There were people who knew my truth first hand because their creations had the ability to carry even a droplet of their sweat or a few discarded cells to my home.

I knew, the next time someone said, "If you hadn't provoked him as a wife, you would not have had this problem. You would still be together," that others quietly knew the truth.

Everyone seemed to have a snippet of wisdom. People suggested that the remedy for marital strife was to "focus only on your issues and ignore Frank's." While there was a truth in that, one of my main issues was allowing myself to be hurt. I needed to work on that first, which meant not ignoring the abuse.

I struggled with the incredulous nature of what had happened in my life. I was so sure that it could not have possibly happened, that it just seemed so surreal. In the end, it was Frank that told me as if he was trying to reassure me, "I really did it." He was still there, the man who beat and raped me. In a way, he was confirming my reality, my sanity, but he was also boasting and taking credit for his work.

#35. POLICE

I have always appreciated police officers, but I did not always think it was safe to turn to them. Frank spent his lunch break going running with a few of them. He told me that I could not get help from them because if I tried and called 911 it would be his friends that came. Some of that might have been a lie, but it muddled my judgment none the less.

Frank always had an angle he was playing to look good. I know at least one of his friends, a probation officer, knew about the abuse and at least some of the details but did not feel it was important to report.

It was interesting, on the outside Frank mastered the role of looking good in the game of reformation. He seemed to enjoy looking virtuous because he was "repentant." Yet he did not stop controlling, isolating, intimidating, or abusing the girls and me.

#36. ON MY OWN

When we separated, I learned how to be by myself. Or more accurately, how to never be by myself. Whether I was getting the mail or rolling over in bed, there were four children with me. One night I woke up pinned by four little bodies on my full-sized bed. I had one on each arm and one on each leg, and I had to pee.

#37. SIMPLE SOLUTIONS

People said it would be awful trying to raise four daughters alone without the help of their father. But as much as I tried, I could never find a day that was harder because he wasn't there. Being able to rest in safety made everything easier.

Instead of having to deal with major problems, little annoyances that fill every young mother's life kept me busy, at least on the days they were with me.

Christy began experimenting. There was not a makeup palette or household liquid too sacred for her lab. I ended up making her a chemistry table OUTSIDE.

Monthly, I vacuumed out the heating vents so that the Cheerios didn't block all the furnace's efforts.

I found worms in the medicine cabinet. Ashley had decided they needed an indoor apartment, complete with furniture.

Finally, I was gaining a bit, paying off my deep debt of exhaustion, but it took me much longer to feel safe.

When I heard people talk about hearing God, I would whisper, "I would rather hear You, and Your presence, for real. In ways through my body than in someone else's way. But I am not sure how to do that because my body doesn't seem like a safe place to live. I'm scared to be touched, even by accident. I'm scared of being hurt in this world. I'm afraid I might do something wrong and cause the abuse to begin again." It has been a long and arduous process.

#38. RECOVERING

As I faced my fears of the abuse starting again, I began to reach out to women who understood my situation. I met at the park with a friend whose husband choked her and beat her children. I went to a secret women's group for women who were in violent relationships. I found a counselor who was willing to take $2 a session for payment. I joined a church that was willing to have my kids in their daycare free of charge so that I could go to those counseling appointments. I cried. I shared little bits of what had transpired in my family. I did something novel; I let myself be cared for instead of just relying on knowledge to make it all make sense.

#39. POSTPARTUM DEPRESSION

My diary reads, "I joined a class on Postpartum Depression. I learned that bowls are better than towels when kids vomit. I learned some other things, too, that I will need time to understand my life. I need my supports and demands to balance. My approach to each day influences me and my kids. But the most important thing I learned this week is that there is hope and caring people hidden in this community who offer refuge from trauma."

#40. INTELLIGENCE

People have asked me if my children get their intelligence from me. It's true. I can be smart, and the girls most likely get their spatial skills from me. Frank could never load luggage into a car. On the other hand, he was anything but dumb. He knew how to plan and how to think ahead as long as it served him. A person cannot be that manipulative and cunning and not be incredibly smart. After all, it takes insight to guard one's appearance in town despite being an abusive man within the walls of one's home. It was one of his strengths that I had to learn and find time to develop. One of the strengths I had to balance with just healing. There is intelligence in planning, but there also is wisdom in learning to breathe and quiet one's self.

#41. ASKING FOR PEACE

God, I can't find any quiet
just to be, just to think
Or even to be simply
At peace

It's so loud in my home
With so many
Needs and demands
Diapers, spit ups, and spills
How can I find our old quiet?
Is there maybe just a little
Heaven could spare?

#42. A SPLIT-SECOND BREATH

God, are you able to split even my heart beats?
Would you try? To stop time
I hope it is not too selfish to ask

God, please find space
Between each beat of my heart
To make infinite silence
The amount that I need
Before my world
Starts back up, loud again

Please be the silence
I can't seem to find
It's desperately needed
To quiet my mind

God, just remember
When my heart beats so fast
Remind me that then
There in those moments
You're meeting my need
Providing more
Silence

And those other times
When my heart

Crawls

Trying to stop

Help me come back

To this world

Full of volume

Woo me to let go

Loosen my grip

And wait to behold

Your eternal relief

Use my heart's gentle beats

To keep me tethered

Balanced between

Life's stressors

And peace

Remember

Your silence

In my heart

It beats

#43. PROBLEMS

Just when everything seemed to be getting better, things would happen to upset the balance. I learned to be okay when events imposed themselves upon my day.

A snowstorm took out the power for days. I went to the local "baby bank," a place that provided clothes and food to low-income families. They stocked us up with instant snacks: granola bars, juice boxes, crackers. I also got four little snowsuits and an old, used doll house. I put out a collapsed box on the snow, and we had a picnic. Thinking back, I wonder if we would have had as much fun without the power going out. Would we have just stayed inside to avoid the cold? I don't know.

After that, we had "power out" nights once a week, playing board games by candlelight. It saved money, and the girls liked it.

#44. MORE OF GOD

In my heart, I cried out to God and heard my response:

> I want to feel You, touch You,
> Even more than I do now. I don't know how.
> It's okay. I want to feel you, touch you,
> Even more than I do now, too.
> We'll find a way.

#45. RESPITE

When the nights got too much and we needed safety, I took the girls to the house of a friend. We slept on her bunk beds. The house was small, less than 1000 sq. ft., but it had enough love for her and her husband, their five children, and me with two of mine. As I struggled with the story of our abuse, she would take me for long car rides while her kids watched mine. She listened and offered the best of advice. She spoke silence.

#46. ADVICE

You are the Counselor, the One who sits with me and makes sense of my past. And if You don't know, "Ask a midwife," You say. "They stand between life and death and always know."

My friend, the one with five kids, was a midwife. It seemed like I could ask her questions without even speaking. She knew to watch my body and how it was responding to stress.

When she visited my home, she commented on the fingerprints and kiss marks my children had left on the mirror. She suggested that I not wash them off; someday those marks would mean more than a messy house and dirty mirrors.

#47. A PENNY A PAGE

I tried to be creative in motivating the girls. I promised them a penny for each page that they read. After a month, I had to stop. They were reading over $20 a month in pennies. Since then, Ashley and Becca both told me that it was that solution that got them hooked on reading.

#48. FLOUR

Becca and Ashley got into 40 lbs. of flour and covered our house while I was nursing Christy. My heart dropped into my stomach when I saw them. Flour painted their bodies white from head to toe. They managed to get some in every room of our home. Finally, I corralled them outside.

Once the excitement of running around wore off, they realized it was in their eyes. I tried using a hose to spray it off. Who knew that washing flour off with a hose would make paper mache paste on their scalps? It took weeks to get it out of the entire house.

#49. THREAT LEVEL

I am struggling
with the intensity
reality
of world events

I can't read the paper
or watch
the news
It's all just too much

I wait to see
a flag at half mast
like me

#50. STOP EVERYTHING

We sit
Blowing bubbles
Rolling balls
It's all okay

You know you have been traumatized when you have to settle the fear of getting hurt in the midst of floating bubbles and small rolling balls. I practiced feeling safe with the things everyone knows could never hurt anyone.

My children helped when Frank was away. I could count on at least one of them doing something absurd. Ashley painted the TV with lipstick because she was following Mr. Roger's lips. Becca asked questions like "How do you spell Latin America?" when she was only 3-years-old. Before I could answer, she would sound it out all by herself even with all the short vowels. Christy was determined to help Elsie learn how to roll over. She repeatedly yanked Elsie's baby blanket out from under her as if she were a magician mastering a trick.

#51. PARADIGM

My husband's therapist said the reason he is still abusing me is that I am too anxious. He told me if I calmed down my anxiety, it would not trigger Frank to be abusive. What a load of crap. People do know that fear is valid when it comes up with a real threat, right? Anxiety only becomes a mental illness when reality does not substantiate it. Anxiety in situations that lead to injury and pain is healthy. My anxiety does not trigger Frank; he exploits my anxiety as his current excuse for being abusive.

When people are around me and anxious or afraid, I don't lash out at them and beat them or tell them they are bad friends and must prove that I am still special by gratifying me sexually while being hit or called names. I listen. I give them space. I might offer something to make THEM feel better, not MYSELF. Only a sociopathic narcissist would use someone else's anxiety as an excuse to hurt them."

#52. THE CHEERIOS

Cheerios cover everything
The couch
The table
Hidden in the potty seat
Stuck to slippers
In the closet

My friends' homes
Didn't have that problem
Their secret
Dogs

Not only do dogs
Listen to kid's secrets
They are masters
At playing hide-and-go-seek
With Cheerios

#53. UNFAIR

Christy takes her medicine
Crushed into a powder
And mixed
With applesauce

Why should she

Be required
To taste bitterness

Without the trauma
Would she even need it
To temper her responses
And help her fears

#54. THE OCEAN

From my diary, "I went to the beach with my grandma today. She got stuck in the sand. Thank You for these chances to forget the abuse. To live life as if it is not happening. Thank You for making moments where I can just be, even though I know the abuse will not end today nor tomorrow. Thank You for making my grandma seem dumb enough for Frank not to keep me from being with her. She knows more than anyone how much I need the freedom just to have a beautiful day."

My grandmother had been in an abusive marriage for decades before my grandfather died of lung cancer. We never talked about it or about what was going on in my marriage, but she was always there to do things. After my grandfather died, she had a second youth. She danced and drank at bars. She drove a purple car way too fast. She inspired me to believe that there could be "life after Frank."

I still remember a week before she was released from her second youth. An ambulance had come to take her to the hospital. When the EMT asked her age, she said 32. Then he questioned my mom, "does she honestly think she's 32 or is she playing with us?" To which a shout came from my grandmother's bedroom, "Don't you dare tell them, Clarie. Maybe one of them will ask me out!"

#55. LOSS

With the approach of winter, I lost three of my closest friends to cancer. Part of me wanted to grieve, to stop everything and reflect on their impacts on my life, but I couldn't. Resting was not something I could do. Instead, I breathed, in and out, in and out, imagining that I could hear the song that their spirit had sung to mine.

It felt like giving CPR to a harmonica.

I had to wonder what was so important in Heaven that God needed three people gifted with compassion and empathy more than me. However, their departure forced me to reach out and ask for help, once again. As usual, it backfired. But this time, I got caught by people who could hear the truth.

#56. THE LOCKSMITH

One of the first people to hear what was going on in my heart was the AAA locksmith. I called multiple times one week, I locked my keys in the car, in the house, and in the trunk. My stress level was astronomical. I felt like my hands were jittering all the way down to my bones. Each time a different locksmith came. The third one asked me, "Ma'am, I noticed you've locked your keys multiple times. Are you okay? Usually, people do this when something is going on. You don't have to tell me, but are you all right?"

I broke into tears. The three people I loved the most were gone. And while I waged a war with grief, my life left me no opportunities to mourn.

The technician couldn't understand what I said, through the blabbering, but he was the first one who heard, "I am alone, but my husband keeps coming back. I'm scared for my kids."

#57. BUCKLING

I know a lot of people talk about the shame of being raped. But my greatest shame came later. After the police were involved, I wrote a letter begging them to let Frank come home for the holidays, that he was no longer abusive, that he had stopped years before. As I wrote that letter, Frank stood in front of me, between my kids and me. I would have written anything to get him to leave. I would have confessed to murder, terrorism, jaywalking. I would have said the world was purple, or blue, or rectangular. It's something I regret. I lied. I messed up their investigation. I falsely stood for someone who I knew was still dangerous. But in those moments, as my pen pleaded for forgiveness, all I could think of was my kids and making Frank happy before Christmas so that they might get to have peace.

#58. PINNACLE OF PAIN

Upon hearing my story, people often think that the hardest part was over. Yes, Frank would keep coming over as I struggled to accept that he would probably never actually "recover," that abuse was something he chose to do repeatedly. But the hardest part for me was not being beaten and raped. It was not struggling to pull myself away. It was when my children started to show the effects of life with an abusive father.

Frank and I tried all sorts of separation plans for "sharing the children." I was in denial that maybe he had gotten better and the children could be safe. I could not face the fact that he was hurting them, too. I could not figure out a way that protected everyone all the time.

#59. ASKING FOR HELP

At some point, I went to the hospital. I told the social worker about some of the abuse that had been going on. I figured I would be safer at a hospital than anywhere else if Frank found out. I turned out to be a mistaken. Someone had told Frank I was there. He still knew people from when he had worked there as a security guard. He was down the hall from my room as I spoke to the social worker.

Only minutes later he would tell the social worker, "Yeah, she just hates me one minute and loves me the next. She makes this stuff up. It's like she has Borderline Personality Disorder." And with those small comments, he saved his reputation, made people feel sorry for him for suffering with an unstable wife, and condemned me to a misdiagnosis and a filter that excluded all my words.

I made a note to myself that day. Don't ever underestimate this man's reach.

Fortunately, everyone that knew me personally (my counselor, psychiatrist, and friends) knew the diagnosis didn't fit. They might not have known the details of the abuse, but they knew I didn't seek attention or waiver in my convictions. It was his last-ditch attempt to discredit me, but he went too far.

#60. MAKING THE MOST OF AN AWFUL SITUATION

Despite the muscle weakness and migraines, I held it together to parent. I imagined that, at some point, I would be able to take the time to reflect and mourn quietly. For the time being, the best way I could honor my confidants was to love my kids, press on to healing, and persevere. The added stress undoubtedly aggravated migraines and weakness, but for the time all I could do was keep going.

I know migraines are debilitating. However, to spite them, I came up with the following strategies. I noticed that people's speech and inanimate sounds seem to speed up or slow down for the first 10-20 minutes of a migraine. Sometimes focusing on these changes helped me tolerate the noise around me, even though it hurt to hear. I also found that each migraine could be a bit unique, some caused my vision to swell, others were aggravated by instrumental music, sometimes they were exacerbated by words. I know that most people just want a quiet room to sleep (I would have liked that, too), but separating out exactly what was painful meant that I could still do some things.

There were so many things that I could not control during this time. Migraines taught me that controlling my attitude and perspective could make even physical pain and distraction manageable.

I also found out another thing. My kids could be captivated by any video with subtitles. Smart as they were, they were eager to read. I played a lot of foreign movies over the years. It didn't matter if it was Japanese or Yiddish, they would sit transfixed decoding the words on half volume with captions.

#61. WHY NOT JUST TAKE A PILL

Before doctors knew that half of my body could get weak with a migraine, they tried using Triptans (medications that stop migraines before they fully develop). The commercials on the TV warn that these should not be used with certain antidepressants, but my doctors figured it should be fine.

What happened with my next migraine? I was at the library with my kids for story time. I took the Triptan as the doctor suggested and got everyone in the car to go home. During the drive, the medicines started to fight.

The road began to look like a river and the power lines like dangling snakes. Nothing new added, but what was there was transformed. It was freaky. Let me remind you, I had taken a migraine abortive medication, not pain pills that caused hallucinations.

I called the psychiatrist's crisis nurse who suggested I try visualization to relax AFTER I informed her where I was, what was going on, and what I was seeing! I am not joking. Sometimes people think they are being helpful when they are blindly quoting off information they learned in school, but they lack any discernment to know if the theory or suggestion is applicable to the situation at hand. There are so many problems with that. I know she was doing her best and would imagine that she could not hear my need through my alarm.

> First, just for safety
> I would have wanted her to
> Suggest a cab
> A friend that could drive
> Or the police

But NO

Instead
Visualize an ocean, a flower
Something to help me calm down
With four kids sitting behind me
Yelling, throwing snacks
Car whizzing by
With people not wanting to share
The road with a person
Hallucinating the road like a river

The part of my brain responsible for
Visualizing crap
Was not the problem
I was seeing lots of "peaceful" images
Just fine

Her next suggestion
Deep breathe
Sitting there
On the side of the road
I pondered
How long can this lady last?
I breathe and decide
I'm just going to drive
The ten miles home

I stopped our conversation

Just write it in the file

I can call the doctor on Monday

Just state

"The road looks like a river

The wires like snakes"

That the medication combo stinks

With the realization that the cars kind of seemed like boats, I could figure out their speed and pretend they were cars, I got home.

When the medicine wore off, the hallucinations stopped. I didn't have a migraine, but I was pissed enough to trigger a new one. Both the neurologist and psychiatrist knew about the other one's drugs.

I called the neurologist, first. His response, "It's true, those medications are theoretically contraindicated, but usually it is fine. Don't take the migraine medicine again."

Well, a theory once validated usually contains some damn good arguments. There was no way I would have tried the two medications together again, not ever.

The next week, I met with the psychiatrist and shared my experience including his crisis nurse's ideas. He got all excited. Seriously.

"We induced an LSD trip. Just imagine what all those dopamine type 2 receptors were doing..."

I sat there, waiting, for him to come down from HIS high. The dangers of driving high on migraine medicine and antidepressants, with four kids in the car, and he was excited? Not to mention that, clearly, my judgment had been impaired. "You realize my life is not a board game to be played, right?"

I wanted to scream, "FOCUS," as I sat there and wondered, how many drugs did this guy do in college? I don't get it. How can there be so many insane doctors in this field? From now on, I will trust the pharmacist.

#62. DEFENSE

It was challenging to feel supported with the isolation that came from care-giving for infants and the safeguards Frank took to make sure I didn't talk. I'm sure I was an enigma to people. It was so hard to process everything that had happened and was still happening.

People we had known for years, seemed to take sides. With Frank's connections at church, he was able to bolster his team. I was conflicted, I could not yet open up about what had gone on or what was still happening. I just tried to wait it out. Wait out people's reactions, hurtful words, and judgments. I didn't know what else to do.

I probably would have been better off shouting or defending myself, but I didn't want to hurt others as they were hurting me. I knew they only had half the story. It is easy to judge women escaping abuse, and their emotional responses, when you don't know the reality of what has transpired. I doubt many people would risk separation and divorce from an abusive partner without a significant reason.

But there was another thing at play: I was used to being blamed for the problems in our marriage. Frank could turn anything and make it my fault. When he lost a job for looking at pornography while on the clock, it was my doing. His reasoning: we were not having sex enough. Multiple times per day was not sufficient to keep his addiction silenced for work.

I agree that if you have to beat someone into submission or terrify them until they give you sex to avoid being punished, it probably does not meet your need for affection. But, MY FAULT? He had to justify it to others. He had to have them feel sorry for him, with all the young children at home. Sympathy for a sociopath, it's like gasoline for a fire.

One thing I believe is important to point out is that abuse by a partner is not just about men abusing women.

Anyone can abuse
Literally ANYONE
Who is insecure or deranged

Abusers can be men or women
Straight or gay
They can be poor or rich
They can claim any religion
Or cling to atheism
They can take drugs and drink
Or be substance virgins
Their skin can be any color
Their eyes any color
They can be in their youth or already retired
They can have any nationality

Abusers are terrorists
In their homes
And once you separate
They can remain
Terrorists

#63. ANTICIPATION

When Ashley was little, she insisted on riding her scooter through the house. In the morning, I would hear her swish-thud through our home. It made me smile to think of seeing her each time. But I also anticipated Frank coming over.

I adopted a cat that seemed to know when Frank was coming. Frank hated cats, but this one instinctively knew that. He would come to the door after Frank left and requested to be let out about five minutes before Frank's car would pull up in front of our home. My cat gave me peace; I knew as long as he was there, I was safe and didn't have to worry about Frank's car in the driveway.

#64. THE VEIL OF NORMALCY RIPPED

Ashley was the first to break from the stress. Not by breaking down, but by trying to keep everyone safe.

#65. DOMESTIC VIOLENCE AND SEX OFFENDER TREATMENT

The signs of abuse and rumors of our separation forced Frank's hand. However, Frank turned everything into an offense. He volunteered to do domestic violence treatment, and sex offender treatment, with the caveat that I never share what had happened.

At one point, the counselor who ran the sex offender group invited me to come to his office for an appointment. After my experiences with Frank's previous counselors, I was weary. He said something that I will never forget. "It's okay to eat a bit of a candy cane."

The sentence sounded so benign, and I doubt the counselor said it strategically. It was near Christmas, there were candy canes, and I could have one. But his words showed me something else: it was okay to relax and enjoy something sweet. I would be okay. I could relax; I was safe there. He got it.

My husband had beaten me for eating when he had not heard my stomach growl. He purposely kept me from food and laughed as I desperately tried to eat. This situation was not like that.

Talking with that counselor was refreshing. I didn't have to explain what it was like to live with a man set on controlling every part of my life. I could relax, if only for a few minutes.

#66. BOUNDARIES

My neurologist explained to me that the best thing I could do for my migraines would be to get divorced. He doesn't even know about the head injuries; he was just talking about the constant stress. It was interesting to think about divorce being an act of self-care, like eating well, getting enough sleep, and staying calm. It was not my natural way of looking at things, but I could see his point.

#67. REINCARNATION

I would never
Wish for an abuser
To have to suffer the pain
They lashed out

The strengths needed

To overcome that injustice

Are too similar

To the strengths needed

To not abuse

Others or power

In the first place

My fear would be this

They would be snagged

By abuse

Unforgiving and bitter

Stuck in that pain

Forever

#68. REVENGE

I have no desire to force

Him to experience what I felt

Whether for a lifetime or a few years

Any more than I would care

To experience his body

And mind

For a single day or hour

That experience

Living with the blind compulsion

To use people without regard

That would injure my spirit far worse

Than any physical pain

Could ever do to him

#69. NAÏVE

People say
I'm too smart ever to be in abuse
I can protect myself with money and brains
But violence affects
The destitute as well as millionaires
Some of its victims had great educations
Others left school unable to read
It doesn't matter

Open your eyes
To a truth
The reason you haughtily say
I would never
Is because the truth
Everyone is vulnerable
To being abused
Is scary
It feels safer to trust
Denial

#70. THE BOND

An abuser
Holds many cards
In the game
Marriage

Power to decide
When you hurt
When you live
When you die

They hold
How people perceive you
When relief comes
The safety of your loved ones
And pets

Keeping them happy
Meeting demands
You might
Be okay for
A bit

The most addicting relief
Inconsistent reward
What happens
They give and decide
Life

You want
Them happy
You want
To feel safe

But that is up
To them

Entirely dependent

Other things
Offer an out
A brochure in a bathroom
The police asking questions
Family concern
But
You ask yourself
Does the escape
Have the power
To play against
One
Who plays as a god
A formidable foe
Who can take
Life
Without blinking
What would be
The cost
Of that

There are very few things that I have seen rip a woman from abuse.
1. Knowing her value
2. Protecting her children
3. An entire community united at once

#71. BUT WHY DOESN'T SHE GET IT AND LEAVE

Gambling at a horse track
Which horse do you back?
The one who consistently outruns all the rest
The one who comes late
Or do you chance fate

Staying or leaving
Forcing you to gamble
But this time it's not money
It's your life

#72. ESCAPES

Sometimes I wished I could drink, but I lost my ability to process with even one glass. Wine, that's something I could not afford. It might only cost a few dollars of money, but it would be like paying a robber to clean out my house. I had to be alert. I had to think and figure out a plan for a way out. I'd rather escape this man's grip permanently than pay alcohol to escape mentally for a mere night.

#73. TRUST

A friend recommended that I try pot. Great idea, huh? Use something that would make me loopy, not care, and eat like crazy. I think not. I'd rather face my life, pain enfolded, than trust a drug like that.

#74. FAMILIES

It seems families always grieve, why can't we just get our child to leave? But the truth, reality is harsh and intense. It can feel unbearable to deal with even a single bit of pressure more.

Let me see if I can find an analogy, since I like to think in pictures and words just don't suffice.

> A circuit breaker blows
> And has to be flipped
> When the draw of current
> Exceeds what's safe
> Hearts and brains blow, too
>
> A cookie sheet
> From the freezer
> In an oven
> Can snap
> The starkness of love
> To abuse
> Snaps pain to your core
>
> Food poisoning and
> An emetic
> Control
> Vomiting
> Being told what to do
> By an abuser

By family
Undermine
Any possible sense of
Agency
The same

#75. IT'S JUST CAUSE AND EFFECT

You stay; he hurts you
You stay more; he hurts you more
Just fucking wake up and leave!
But
You don't realize
Abuse victims have radar
For emotions that precede getting hurt
Frustration
Irritation
Annoyance

When you come
Enter the house
Judging
Annoyed
You might
Have uniforms and be police
Or be family bonded through time
You might
Have pulled her abuser off of her
Twenty times

You might need to
Cry as you finish your shift
Or stumble to bed
But she senses
Irritation
Annoyance
Your feeling of helplessness

You can't make yourself
Not feel
You can't
Get her to believe
She deserves more
She doesn't have to live like this
But may I suggest
Silence
Your grief and
More importantly
Fold away your critique

There
In that moment
Focus all your intensity as
Kindness
And caring
Not viewing her as
A hopeless case
An annoyance
A failure too dumb to see

Truth
But
A human
One who might die
Later that night

You have two minutes
As she begs to have the abuser stay
Knowing that those words
Might keep her 'til tomorrow
Alive, if not safe

For two minutes
Be a refuge of belief
I don't want this to be the last time
That we see you
In situations like these
I've seen too many people
Die
We got it right now
We are in control, not him
For this moment, you're safe
Safe for a moment

Does it take everything
To not scream
We're all just waiting for you to
Figure this out
Believe in yourself

Trust you don't have to live this way
Imagine though
Your voice is like the teacher's
In Charlie Brown's class
With her backdrop of adrenaline
She can read your pupils
But your words
Sound like wadding up paper
Get it together
It's basic deduction
You're an idiot
You must like being beaten
Don't you have the brains
To take control of your life
Why the hell are you so bent
On protecting that ass

It does
It takes strength
To shut up
And help her pull back
From the fear
Gaining traction
To think

#76. TRAUMA BRAIN

I have had people ask me why I didn't see the connection between staying with Frank and suffering more abuse. It is a hard question to answer. To which I suggest:

>Imagine your memories
>Were captured on slides
>All ordered
>Recording your life
>And as a child, you learned
>Simple logic
>Cause and effect
>It's a simple
>Induction
>But abuse
>It takes all your slides
>And dumps them into an unsorted
>Mess
>
>You pick one up
>It is kind
>Another shows danger
>You drop it
>And recoil
>Is it wise to keep
>Picking them up?
>Can you put them in order when

Trauma and terror
Disable all thought
Cause and effect
Future injury
It's here at this moment

There is a reason
People jump out
Of the window
Escaping a fire
To their death
Time doesn't matter

Right now what
Promises
The least pain
Or impending
Threat

Daring to leave
Challenges
The survivor
Will she have more tenacity to live
Than her abuser has to abuse?

But back to my story...

#77. WORN OUT

The time came
When it was all too much
When I knew
I was too weak
To care for anyone
Friends guarded my kids
Adopting them in
To their families
For just over
Two months

Ashley was in kindergarten
Becca and Christy preschool
Elsie less than a year old

I tried to recover
I tried to think
I tried to
Pull it together

Between Frank
Dropping in
Promising reform
I didn't know
What to believe
What I could do

I couldn't yet think
I missed my kids
Without breastfeeding
My milk dried up
My breasts withered
My heart shrank

"Mommy, are you okay?"
Christy cried
When she saw me
Awakening
My will

Next I did something
Only God could inspire
I went to the store
And bought two boob
Enhancements?
Bags like jelly
They felt real
And I
Let God
Help me
Wear motherhood
Again

Was I better?
Facing the truth
When I gave my girls

Hugs
They were padded
Props softening the blow
Working as crutches
Or comforts
'Til my mind
Had time to grow

By March, the girls were back home with me. They were terrified I would get sick again, and they would have to stay with friends.

Slowly, they drew into their old routines. Ashley's "adopted family" still came by to take her to school, going out of their way to help for the rest of the school year. Getting a break, resting, helped give me the time to get out of the rut.

Unable to figure out how I could use the little energy I had, I needed to:

Keep my girls safe
Plan a way out
And

#78. TERROR

With just a few weeks of kindergarten left, I got sick. That morning, as the car pulled off, Ashley opened the door and jumped out of my friend's vehicle. Her heart would not let her leave me when I was sick. She was terrified that she wouldn't see me for weeks. In her trauma response, Ashley gave up all semblance of safety and clung to me.

Terrified and impulsive, she needed a stability I could not provide and still be human. Sometimes, with the flu, a person looks dragged out and needs to sleep off a fever. I just couldn't fake it, and Ashley didn't care that she could have been hurt or injured jumping out of a moving car. She wanted me.

Knowing what I do now, I would have kept her home and let her rest beside me, read books, and feel bonded. However, all I knew was that she wasn't safe. She was too impulsive for me to manage, and I couldn't fix it. She needed somehow to teach her how to calm her heart.

Not sure how to even keep her buckled in a car, I called Frank for help. It is strange, looking back. Why would I call our abuser for help? And yet, I was used to feeling helpless and vulnerable in his presence. The dynamics of loyalty and need in abuse are bizarre. He drove us to the hospital over 100 miles away, so no one he knew would know. He had to be with us to steer the conversation away from him when she was admitted. She spent a week.

When she was discharged, she was on an antidepressant, had a referral to counseling, and had a diagnosis. All of which led to counseling and counseling for her sisters, which led to occupational therapy and speech therapy, and lots of appointments and support.

Her new counselor tried to explain it to me, "She was terrified of not seeing you again. She equates your presence with survival." But something had happened while she was in the hospital, I lost hope that I could make a difference in the lives of my kids. I started to wonder if they would be better off without me. I could not even get one to the hospital without calling Frank.

#79. START OF A NEW YEAR

The following fall, the school had a plan to help her get to school. By that time, Frank and I were settling into the kids with me during the week and him on the weekends.

With a little more distance, I started to see things clearer. The teachers at Ashley's school said they could not even assess her functioning on Monday or Tuesday because she always seemed to be in shock after weekends with her dad.

#80. MEMORY

God asked me to draw, write, express whatever I could remember.

Gray, I see gray

The cat jumped off the window sill and puked as it went over my face. That's a better memory than being raped in front of a child.

#81. RECOIL FROM PAIN

When I was younger, I made the mistake of playing tag in the kitchen with my grandmother. In an attempt to get away, I ran right into the wood stove. I would have thought that touching something so hot would cause me pull away automatically, but it didn't. I still remember the realization that it hurt more to pull my hands away than leave them on the stove. My skin was melted onto the stove's surface, and I had to rip my hands away. That is a lot like leaving an abusive marriage. It hurts. It felt like I was choosing to tear part of me from my body, but it was paramount that I do it to prevent further injury.

It is strange. In the midst of the abuse, I somehow lost my ability to get anxious. I felt dead to the world and no longer cared if I died from being beaten or raped. I was no longer concerned I would die; I was worried that

I wouldn't and that I would have to live through more. I was also anxious I would have to see my daughters, no longer spectators, experience it, too.

#82. DESPERATION

God, is there an answer
Can we get out of this
And still have a place to live
Safety to sleep
Whom do you have
With discernment
That can get us out
With the skill of a surgeon

#83. LIFE NEVER STOPS

In the midst of my personal family drama, my parents adopted another child. It is interesting how many normal, everyday, beautiful things still happen even in the midst of a personal crisis. My girls called her "baby aunt" for years. Sometimes, she came over during the day and fell asleep as I held her.

Frank never wanted me to bond with the babies. Even when I nursed, he thought they should be put right down in their cribs. My sister was different. I could watch her close her eyes and drift peacefully to sleep.

When I think of her coming and joining our family, I imagined a May Pole with beautiful ribbons woven together. It was as if her first family wrapped her with love and tied a ribbon on her, so that as she crossed oceans and rivers to join us, she wove above us in the sky.

It made me wonder how the Heavens had decided to give me a braid with four strands. Everyone knows, four strands can't be woven into a braid easily. And with that, I saw a flicker of hope. Maybe I could figure that out, even if I sucked as a mom like the counselors seemed to think.

#84. LITTLE THINGS

I had theme nights
Dinner
A movie
Craft
Talking
We watched the Absent-Minded Professor
Made outlines of our bodies on paper
And stapled them to the ceiling
So we could fly
Small
Meaningless
Family things

#85. GLITTER

I hired a girl training to be
A doula to help me with my girls
As I recovered from Elsie's birth

I crashed on the bed
To sleep

An hour of rest
I woke up
To streets of gold

Twelve bottles of glitter
Had been poured out
In every room of
The house

I chuckled inside
Even a teen
With energy intact
Could lose a battle
With my children

Despite sweeping
And vacuuming
Glitter remained

I'd like to see
Child welfare
Wrestle with that
Four kids under four
Without a single
Mess

One of my daughters later wrote me a card, "Thak you for clening the haous." They noticed, even if I was far from perfect.

#86. PNEUMONIA

I went to the doctor today. I feel like I am drowning in water. I asked my doctor to take an x-ray of my lungs, but he said the insurance wouldn't cover it. I am not coughing. I don't have a fever. But I feel so lethargic, and I feel like I am drowning, plus I am craving white wine. I never crave white wine unless I have bronchitis or pneumonia. Everything might lie, but my cravings for food tell the truth. He wasn't convinced, but I refused to leave.

"I'll pay for the x-ray. If I have pneumonia, you can bill the insurance." He ordered an image. I had pneumonia. Insurance covered the x-ray and antibiotics. I knew it. I hate white wine.

At the end of the appointment, I mentioned that my girls had been moving slowly. They had no other symptoms than weakness and fatigue. The doctor had me bring them in, all of them had it, too. No symptoms and no fevers, but we all had active pneumonia.

I wonder if abuse could wear down our defense, our willingness to fight and live. Normal bodies fight, they cough up phlegm, heat up the defenses, tighten the chest. Ours weaken and relax. Defenseless, like they are preparing to die. Doctors are used to looking for the signs of fighting and not the actual disease.

#87. ALARM

The girls came home
From a weekend
With Dad
Becca, a mark
A burn

The size of a cigarette
On her arm

I remember
The call
Reporting
The mark
The response
Child welfare does not
Get involved
In custody battles

During divorce
Either of us could have
Done it
But the truth
I don't care who did it

My kid was hurt
Forget allegiances
Keep my damn kid
SAFE

I was pissed. They insinuated that I had done it for the sole purpose of tainting their imaginary rendition of Frank. Hell, being autistic, I didn't even have a deep enough insight or understanding to pull off that type of crap. I just wanted my kids not to be hurt. Surely, they couldn't throw out every concern?!?

If they even hypothesized that I could have done it to frame Frank, they should have taken the kids out of both of our care to keep them safe. There is a problem when even child welfare is too jaded to keep the kid's interest in mind.

#88. DIVORCE

Divorce wasn't easy. People asked me if I felt guilty for not trying harder. They asked if I wish I hadn't and warned me that my children would suffer from growing up without their father around all the time. They said I was making too much out of his mistakes and not valuing what God had done. Their words were misguided, but they still spoke them.

There was also the challenge of letting go my desire to have the perfect marriage and life. I wanted to be a person known for perseverance and character and was unsure how I could given my situation. But despite all my doubts, and knowledge that the healing would take time and hurt, I knew that I had done the best thing I could, for everyone involved.

#89. THE PULL TO REMEMBER

What do I remember? I remember You.
I remember You sitting with me
When I could only bring myself to see
The cat jumping over my bed
I remember You slowing down
The flashbacks second by second

I remember You breaking my fall

As I collapsed on my bed in tears
I remember You breaking from religion
To clarify your words

I remember You staring back at me as
I wept and blubbered my story
The first time
I remember Your eyes
Your passion
Your hope
That I couldn't see
At the time

#90. CLINGING

Christy
Latches on to me
Refusing to let go
The principal and secretary
Hold her arms and legs as she lay
On the floor
Speaking kindly to her
Just like me

Christy, you are fine
No one is hurting you
Your mom is right here
She's okay
You don't have to freak out

She is going to leave and
You will see her again

They held her and her fears
Despite district policies and guides

That night I wrote, "It is such a relief that they "get it." God, thank You for giving them the courage to not follow the protocols, and to help solely because my daughter and I need it."

#91. ENDURANCE

Sometimes, you just have to hold them
As safely and purposely as you can
Until something changes
Keep working
Keep firing those muscles
Even when they want to stop
Keep focused
There might be a moment
To escape
Don't miss it
Giving up

#92. LA LECHE

Without the support
Of feeling safe even

At church

I turned to midweek times

To meet with women

In groups

#93. MENTORING

One of the moms suggested a book on how to avoid power struggles with kids. It was weird; she didn't seem to have many conflicts with her son. I got the book and discovered why. Unlike most parenting books on how to force kids to obey or motivate them with stickers, this one helped me appreciate my children and their temperaments.

The short version: Kids have personalities. Parents have personalities. Sometimes those personalities clash. My goal was not to make my child like me, or even to make parenting more pleasant for me. My job was to help shape them to be who they are so they can be effective in our society in a way that works for them.

#94. PERSONALITIES

Becca likes to stay up as I read my notes from my "Neuro Psych" class. She poses rebuttals to the lecture notes that I can't answer. My teacher is impressed when I take them to class, but the truth is my preschooler develops the questions.

Ashley convinced her therapist to let her climb trees during her appointment. I looked over from the other side of the park to see her near the top of one, 100 ft. up or so, with her counselor saying "I think that is too far, why don't you head down," over and over. And the wisdom of this counselor is supposed to be enough to navigate withdrawing from an abusive marriage in one piece.

Elsie is fine with anyone holding her. Instead of the usual nine-month clinging, she doesn't seem to notice. I feel conflicted, people comment how calm and content she is and think I should be rejoicing. But I am not. There is a level of health in natural development and phases.

Christy wore Halloween costumes for a year to school. That and a helmet after getting distracted and knocking herself out on the playground.

One of them gave me a note, but I hope the sentiment is true for all of them: "Mom, I may not have been the best kid in the world... but you made me feel like I was. Happy Birthday! Mom, I love you so you are the best mom I could ever have." Being loved by my daughters, and loving them, is what makes us "the best."

If my life's wisdom could be distilled into a single quote, it would be: "Perfection pales in the face of love." -Sophia Grace.

#95. VOCALIZING OUR TRUTH

Christy was the first of the girls to talk about the abuse to me. I should have known that it would be her. Even as a baby, she had a robust vocabulary. At one year of age, she knew over 50 words.

She had asked me for a fairy doll multiple times over the course of two weeks. I had NO money, so I did something illegal. I let her run a lemonade stand with lemon and sugar that I had bought with food stamps. There are only two times in my life when I have done that. This one and another one that we made homemade cookies to be able to purchase school supplies one year. The secret with cookies, we took them to neighbors during a football game. Men loved an excuse for instant sweets and would happily pay a dollar even without a cookie just to get back to the game.

Within a few hours of selling lemonade, she had earned $15, the amount she needed for the Rainbow Fairy. That week, she took her doll to counseling. Her counselor was old school. She didn't tell me what to do; she let my children show me how they felt. As Christy played with her doll and an old doll house, she told the therapist that her doll was "the angel that came at night to take the kids to a faraway place." When the counselor asked, she responded, "That's when the dad is hitting the mom." My ears opened when I heard the voice of my child. There was no doubt, my kids knew.

I had other doctors and counselors try to beat that truth into my brain, but their approach didn't work. One of Ashley's psychiatrists said that he didn't think I was getting migraines. He thought I was just overwhelmed by my husband abusing the kids that I checked out with the excuse of a headache. I considered his insight, but threw it out; I did get migraines. I would have done better if he had said, "You need to ask yourself, are your kids completely safe? Just being in a violent home damages kids for life. Are you willing to risk that? How much violence are you willing to tolerate?"

#96. ONE DARK NIGHT

Not knowing which of Frank's friends could be safe was hard. He had said that none of the police would believe me, that Ashley would say that he was hitting us, just to get him in trouble, and that I had to trust him in all things or I'd be "in trouble." I didn't know to whom I could go. If I went to my family, he could hurt them. If I went to the police, they would put me in line. If I dared talk, I would not talk a second time.

A single police officer changed that. Frank, our kids, and I had just been in the parade with the county judges and commissioners. We looked adorable with all the girls in matching outfits. The perfect family per a camera. Afterward, we went to dinner with the city officials.

I broke a tooth that night, but even that pain did not overwhelm what happened next. When the plates cleared, and we walked outside:

> A lone police car
> Sat
> In the alley by the restaurant
> The window down

There is no way in hell I would have walked over to the car, but the commissioner had no such hesitation. Leading the way, he walked right up and started a conversation. "Thanks for your service tonight. Were you able to enjoy the parade?"

> The officer
> Was crying
> Why?
> He had just left
> A domestic dispute
> Torn up
> Emotionally
> Trying to recover
> To finish out his
> Shift

His tears showed me, he got it and cared. Even standing next to Frank, with four perfect children, and a broken tooth, I saw that some people were not callous to abuse.

#97. A CROWN

Some crowns just can't wait until Heaven.

#98. LETTING GO

I was convinced that if I dared express or even think about the reality of what had happened, and what was still happening, I would die from grief. Slowly, I started to hear, "I will not die from letting it up."

I wrote, "God I am holding on so tightly, trying to make life work, to keep the memories boxed away. I wonder if it would be okay to let a few up, so I don't have to hold so many. Could You slow the flood if they start to whiz by me too fast?"

#99. CONSIDERING DEATH

In the crap of trying to get out of the abuse, I thought about hanging myself, overdosing, dousing myself with gasoline and lighting it, but I never did. When it came down to it, I figured I could be the flare that got help. My dead body would get treatment and help for my kids, and the alarm would show the depth of the girls' needs. But beneath that, I had two fears.

One, I would not succeed, and I would have to lay comatose listening to the hell my children faced in abuse from my husband. And, two, I would succeed and cause the people who did care, my family and the people who sat in cars crying in the dark, to have to carry my pain. I could not do that to them. Honestly, refusing to hurt even people I might never know kept me alive.

#100. HICCUPS

Despite having had three toddlers before Elsie, I still struggled to remember all the details such as: don't take kids for a walk on the day they get shots at the doctor's office. Walking to the store with her and three other children went smoothly, but once we were there I knew I had blown it. Crying and aching, she collapsed to the floor not wanting to walk. Her legs hurt too much, so I got creative.

The store was going through a remodel and was temporarily "strollerless," so I bought a little kid's doll stroller instead. We only had to go seven blocks, but I knew she was too heavy, and I was too weak, to carry her. The toy worked for three blocks and then cracked under pressure. What was nearby? The National Guard Armory. I did what any desperate mom would do, I went in and asked for duct tape.

I started by saying, "Do you by chance have any duct tape I can use?" The man holding down the fort replied, "Yes," before he had the insight to ask, "What do you need it for?" Ten minutes later, I had a doll stroller reinforced by sticks and high-quality tape. All I can say, the National Guard knows how to do a lot with a little. But the part that was even more special, Elsie's sisters got to see a man in a uniform show kindness and concern.

#101. TIME

Coming to grips with all that had happened was a long process. Even being willing to think about acknowledging it was a process.

Marks of abuse
Tenaciously hold
Pain and drama together
To say
We are scars
That cling

As my energy snags
And wanes in their grip
So tight, so harsh
Let them play
Their music so loudly

Their song
Brings release
May it echo its beating
The notes that it's found
And untie
Your rhythm in me

#102. FEARS

I began considering what fears could get in the way of our future. I avoided help when I was weak or hurting, scared that I would be squashed in a vulnerable state.

I feared going out and running into Frank or being seen doing something he wouldn't like. Being stalked by someone who has shown repeatedly that they can hurt you is scary.

The low-income counseling in our town was a place where Frank had worked for years. The assistant director did not think that they could provide counseling and confidentiality given the circumstances, so I saw a counselor in the next county over.

Fitting the theme of my life, I found another solution that was untraditional. I found a group of women online with agoraphobia and let them teach me their techniques for facing the fear of getting out. I wasn't agoraphobic, I had PTSD, but the wisdom of recovery was the same.

#103. GOING BACK TO SCHOOL

I went back to school. I figured I should do something I was good at and diversify my life. I had always been an excellent student, earning A's through high school and my first two years of college. I dropped out and got married before I finished a degree.

It was unbelievable how much technology had changed college. It was easier to write research papers at home with four kids than it was to request interlibrary loans and hard copies of articles. I could just "google" it. The world was at my fingertips. Plus, I had lots of encouragement. Instead of feeling jealous, Christy wrote me a card: "You are the best mom! momo I no how harded it is to be in school."

#104. TOO SLEEPY TO FUNCTION

In the pursuit of my studies, I kept falling asleep. I had always fallen asleep at odd times, even as a child. I fell asleep standing up. I fell asleep in the middle of a conversation. I fell asleep preparing dinner. I even fell asleep during counseling. But my "tiredness" was always blamed upon my life: I had arthritis which could be fatiguing, I had young children, I was a single mom.

One of my professors recommended that I speak to my doctor about a sleep study. I did. It turned out I had narcolepsy and cataplexy. My body had a faulty switch for going to sleep and waking AND I had muscle weakness from intense emotions. The study confirmed what I already knew.

After the doctor looked at the sleep study and gave me the diagnosis, he recommended that I read up on the subject. It turned out that my neurologist had already told him that he thought I had cataplexy. Honestly, I wasn't sure I would be able to read up on narcolepsy and do my reading for school. To which he replied, "I think now that it's treated you'll be surprised at how much easier everything will be."

He was right, I no longer needed to nap for 10 minutes before I drove a few miles. I didn't need to cut up chicken sitting down at the table in case I fell asleep holding the knife. But it was something else that shocked me. I could speak and stand when I was terrified. I could hear jokes and not slouch over instead of laughing like everyone else. I could start to explore the details of the abuse in counseling without needing 30 secs for my slack jaw to function when I remembered the details of abuse. I could speak and use my arms to defend myself.

After a month, I figured that he was right, I should read up on narcolepsy. It clearly had affected my life. I was unsure what I should read. Doctors always seemed to be annoyed by people finding health information online, but I had student access to PubMed and a lot of cool journals through school, so I set aside a night and dedicated myself to reading.

For those who do not know me, I can go through literature like a bulimic goes through food when I find it interesting. After I had read what I could online, I ordered a textbook from Amazon on the psychosocial aspects of narcolepsy.

For the most part, the medication treated the muscle weakness and random sleeping. I could stay awake during lectures. I could drive to the grocery store and shop without randomly falling asleep in the frozen section.

#105. BODIES SPEAK

My kids' bodies
Are worn as well
Chronic stress has
Altered their immune systems
Taxed the delicate balance
Of their glands
Stripped their nerves
And left
Them
Depleted

To those trained to listen, my children's bodies spoke loudly. I had a friend, a massage therapist, who worked on my kids. The first time she helped them, she took me aside.

"I have a serious question for you. I have only felt those patterns of tension in people who have experienced abuse or sexual assault. I don't know your story, but it's alarming."

#106. HOLDING A FRANTIC KID

One of the suggestions
For Ashley by her therapist
Was for me to "hold her"
When she freaked out
Until she calmed down

Eventually
A traumatized kid
Will give up
Kicking and screaming
And rest

Maybe that is true
For some kids
But not for Ashley
Without even a
Fundamental sense
Of safety

She would
Fight
As if for
Her life

#107. THE BRUISES

I am clothed with bruises
Pieced together by
A child
Flailing while I held her
Asleep now

I go to my bed
Trying
Don't cry
I swore I would never
Sleep with bruises
Ever

Again

Another day, teach her
To be calm, centered, and free
Just don't think of the
Bruises
They are hurting
Me

#108. THE ATIVAN

Stored in the fridge
A prescription

Ashley's souvenir from the hospital

A bottle of Ativan

So bitter

She would never take it

I found a use for it today

The fourth of July

A year later

The dog freaked out

By noise

Now lies asleep

There was no way I would have ever touched it. I had an antianxiety drug once in the hospital and thought the world was fucking dissolving. My anxiety responses better to things that keep me awake, alert, and able to function, not a false sense relaxation or peace.

#109. WEEKENDS

The discrepancy of having to send them with Frank, knowing they are with him for two nights—I can't deal with it. As a mom, to send your kids with their abuser and know that you are not there to redirect the abuse to yourself. It's enough to crack someone's brain. People tell me I should rest up, energizing my body for Sunday night, but my spirit wretches inside me the entire time they are gone.

How do you do that? How do you rest when your heart is crying out? SCREAMING in your chest. THEY ARE NOT SAFE. How do you rest then? How do you take up a hobby and relax? The only way I could rest would be, well, to be dead.

I told that to my doctor; now, I'm in the hospital with a mandatory hold. Which means, you guessed it, the kids are with him this WEEK. Note to self: there are some things not to tell a doctor. In the hospital, the social worker informed me that child welfare would not look well upon a mom who tried to commit suicide. I guess they look better on sending kids to stay with a rapist.

Do you want to know the great ideas the psychiatric ward had? Put me in group therapy with an insane man describing stalking his girlfriend and how he wanted to hurt her. When I took care of myself by leaving the group and sitting in the common area, the chart notes said I was refusing to engage in group therapy. For some reason, listening to psychotic and jealous ravings was not therapeutic for me.

That night when they moved him to the room next to mine, I could not sleep. Imagine that. I took my blanket and laid down on the floor in front of the nurses' station. The next morning, the doctor decided I must be bi-polar because I "was agitated and unable to sleep" according to the night shift.

The doctors took me off the antidepressant that was treating the cataplexy and put me on a mood stabilizer. As any neurologist would know, if you suddenly stop a medication that treats cataplexy, the patient's cataplexy gets much worse. The chart notes at that point: patient does not even answer questions, lies there without moving.

There I was at the doctors' mercy waiting for them to stop being IDI-OTS or at least read an idiot's guide to trauma and sleep disorders. After I was released, my sleep medicine doctor wrote them a letter AND sent them a copy of my sleep study detailing the effects of refusing to treat narcolepsy and cataplexy. My counselor wrote a letter differentiating between utter shock and trauma and bipolar mania. What did I write? I wanted to send them an envelope full of horse poop, but instead I decided just to be grateful that people were willing to put their necks on the line to keep me as healthy and well as they knew how.

#110. HOME

I got home and
Collapsed by the dining room table
And slept
As far from their bedrooms
And the doctors
As possible

#111. 'TIL MORNING

Another night I wrote:

I crept to the baseboard
The floor
Tonight, in the doorway
Snuggled by the dog
I can't sleep
My house
The rooms
The walls
Echo pain
Like drums

One night at a time
I hope. I wait
The sun will come up
And with it
Maybe
My fear
Defeat

#112. SUNRISE

When I was little, my dad would wake me up. Three words, "Sophie, it's morning." I have always kept the tradition, but now God wakes me up with the sun and not my father's voice.

#113. LIKE A POP-UP CARD

Memories have a way of
Popping up in my mind
They used to be scary
Like goblins
Popping up in a
Haunted house
Now I think of them
As paper cut out in a card
I try to pretend
It's God teaching me
Not to jump

When I see what
Frank did

Slowly, it's helping. I can tolerate little pieces. Even though memories come up, I know that paper never lasts forever. Even the rain can dissolve its power. And if the rain never came, a fire would do. And if that seemed to miss, I can count on my final friends, worms and termites. The memories reduced to a little ink.

#114. NARCOLEPSY

One thing that took me a long time to come to grips with was the impact of narcolepsy on being abused.

Incapacitated
Even to scream
No strength to
Push him off

I try to get help
To say what is
Happening
But my mouth
Refuses to move

But that is not
The worst part
The narcolepsy
Confuses my mind

It paralyzes me
Just a bit

When I go to sleep
When I wake up
Sleep paralysis
Shouldn't matter
Right?

But waking up
To rape
Falling asleep
Unable to move
Narcolepsy forcing
My mind to dream
While I am still
Awake

Because of the narcolepsy and cataplexy, I could not scream. I could not push him off my body. When I asked for help I had to deny every emotion to think without feeling. There were many ways that narcolepsy affected me.

People with narcolepsy can have hypnogogic and hypnopompic hallucinations; our brains play dreams as they experience REM sleep while we are still awake. The hallucinations aren't psychotic; they can actually be exacerbated by antipsychotics. They are treated with antidepressants that interfere with deep sleep. Without treatment, the hallucinations occur when we fall asleep and wake up.

The sleep paralysis is exactly what it sounds like. When we fall asleep and wake up, we can be totally awake for a few minutes before we can command our bodies to move at all.

Imagine, because I still can't say this in first person, that you wake up being raped by your husband. You can't move, do anything, or even roll over, but your mind is fully awake. Imagine on top of that, having your brain in dream mode, hallucinating ON TOP of the terror of being raped.

If that isn't enough, imagine telling a social worker when asked "Have you ever had hallucinations?" "Yes, I have narcolepsy," and not realizing that she doesn't even have the training to know you are not talking about psychosis. Imagine being taken off the effective medication and, instead, being given one that makes it worse. You are only left with the power to breathe and keep it together until you are released.

#115. SOCIOPATHS

I tried to figure out how what happened to me could be labeled coercion, I felt ill to my stomach when I looked up the definition. I tried reading BDSM pornography rationalizing that it contained similar themes: punishment, control, domination, and perversion. I never even knew that stuff existed. All I could ask myself was why didn't Frank find someone into that crap? Maybe because it wouldn't have been as fun to manipulate, control, and torture. It would have denied him the ability to show the full scope of his power, plus the pornography for those things don't include children. I'm sure it exists somewhere; our society is screwy enough for sure. Trying to view it or understand it from the perspective of a sociopath, especially being autistic, is way more than I could figure out with logic.

I finally resigned myself to this conclusion: sociopaths like to hurt people, they like to control people, and the good ones are hard to spot.

#116. DETERMINATION

Even without understanding sociopathic reasoning, I needed to deal with a more pressing issue. I had to find the strength to keep trying.

I set aside a little note to stay focused: "I will figure this out. I will figure out what in the hell to do. I will be like a poor black woman in Chicago during the depression; I will find the resources I need to get through this, alive. And, I will be bringing four kids with me. Alive and, someday, healed. And that jackass will not have hurt my family nor will he have succeeded in silencing me. I don't care if I have to figure out how to speak with inflection, have people hear me, or wear a lavender tutu for a year. I will make it through this."

#117. A MOMMA"S LOVE

When something is wrong, moms will do whatever we can to find an answer. It's what my mom did. She was aggressive in the face of danger, she fought, she sacrificed herself, and she didn't give up.

If we, as moms, see that we are not protecting our children with our current approach, you better damn well believe that any threat will be taken out. It may take a group effort. It may take all of society working in unison. It may take a lot of time, but we will get it done or die trying.

#118. RULES IN THE SANDBOX

One of the things I had to set aside, so that I could recover, was all the rules I had made up about God, how to live, and what other people expected of me. Occasionally, I will have a well-meaning Christian think I need to be saved, because I didn't write "Jesus is ALL anyone needs to be saved and go to Heaven" fifty times in this book. I love Jesus. I know He is how I got through this, but being religiously perfect (and having a slew of impeccable, theoretical arguments) did not get me out of abuse. It took God, a lot of awesome people, and time to get out of such an awful situation.

So, if you are one of the readers who is so blinded by religion that you cannot accept that humans do not have to be perfect (i.e. that you still need to rely on God to go to Heaven and not your own perfection), put this book down and write God a letter, not me. I am very aware that Jesus is real. I have purposely not cleaned up my story to be politically and religiously correct. Being imperfect is what has allowed me the opportunity to heal in the hands of an all perfect God.

> God hates statues
> Or so I was once told
> But He chose one
> To help me
> Just one alone
>
> Before me a tray
> Filled with sand
> A companion beside
> With training and love
> Fill your life
> What is there
> It's just a tray of sand
> An area of protection
> Guarded by gems

An invisible gate
But
In the center
Nothing
A thief's words
Once ate

My power
My passion
My role as a mother
My honesty as a daughter
My life
My fate

I sat there
Staring
Grieving the loss
The words:
I wasn't helping
It was my fault
Just leave
You're rejecting
Don't sit at our table
Emotionally-absent
Twisting Frank's image
Everything sounding
Like the dongs of
Cinderella's
Midnight clock

Sophia Grace

My esteem
Made worthless

But instead of leaving
The session that day
I returned to the shelves
And on them displayed
A statue

Most people would
Think
I'd pick Jesus, a cross
I could have, but that
Was not what I needed
I needed a symbol
Of motherhood and strength
A symbol of caring
And nurturing

The pain
Caused
By words
The doctors
The psychiatrists
The teachers
My friends
My church
Even family
Spoke

Unsupported

To ears, only heard

Dialects of

Autism

They didn't speak that

Language

Though they would if they'd known

So filling the center

I sat down

Kuan Yin

A mother of compassion

Of quiet grace and reflection

The truth of my strength

Representing not God

But me

Reflected

By faith

#119. THE POWER OF PRAYER

I have often stated, "There is no wrong way to grieve." Apart from addiction, I imagine there is no wrong way to heal, either.

I know

I do not listen to

The ways people speak

As most can

I hear uniquely

Guttural and raw

Unrefined

But I can't see

The need

To buffer

God

In prayer

There is a power

In honesty

That cannot be found

Piecing together scripture

Like a

Ransom letter

No one

Buffers me

And I am no better

Than God

#120. PRUDENESS

My mother once said, "Any Bible that cannot handle a little spilled food is not worth being trusted to handle life." Another one of her favorite sayings is "Talk never cooked rice."

So, God, are You as prude as people say? There are so many things I need to talk about, but people act like You will break if You hear them. I need You to heal the rip in my heart.

How can you do that without abuse's kryptonite stopping my soul?

The things abuse donned:
Prayer and religion
Domination, control
Phrases of counseling
It is like being sick
And allergic
Antibiotics can battle
But not in that case
God, I am sick
But I can't heal the ways
That usually work

Let me be blunt
Are You as prude as Your church?
Are You as sheltered and guarded as most people think?
Do You care more about which hole
A penis penetrates
Than the hearts of the people involved?

By the way, God
If You try to pull any of the Old Testament crap
About husbands forcing their wives to abort
A CHILD
Because they are paranoid that she had an affair
Save your breath. Don't even go there
So where does that leave You?
Time. Healing takes time.

There are so many topics that seemed too unholy for God, but those were the topics that were binding me. I needed the freedom to speak to God about violence, sex, abuse, fear, judgement, religion, and hundreds of topics too awful for hour long sermons but not too awful for God. I set aside all my prayer rules and just started to talk about everything: my kids, what confused me, how pretty the clouds were... it didn't matter. I was the one who got to decide how prude I would be with God. Any topic I could talk about, He could hear. After all, He had heard all of Frank's words when he beat me and nothing could be more offensive than that.

#121. AGGRESSION

Children often pick up the mannerisms of their parents and mine were not immune. I wrote the following in my journal:

"Ashley is being aggressive with her sisters. I am separated from their dad, but his behaviors are being replayed by my oldest. I like Elsie's way better; she kills Lego people weekly in therapy. All sorts of violent deaths. In my desperation, I called Child Welfare. Their solution is to have her stay with her dad since none of the allegations have resulted in charges. Sure, he was required to take domestic violence and sex offender therapy, but he got a deal that spared him the title "sex offender" so he must be safe. It doesn't matter that his behavior torments and terrifies Ashley. He is willing to take her and family always chosen before foster care." Since I had said Ashley was not safe with her sisters, my hand was forced. She had to live with her dad until she was stabilized.

A month later I saw her when her father brought her to the doctor. She had been sick with the swine flu for two weeks, but he still sent her to school. She had gained a lot of weight. She no longer cared about life and had no fight in her at all. Seeing a child broken is a tragedy. I don't care if they have been aggressive or not.

#122. WEAKNESSES

Obviously, my life was not working. My strengths weren't enough, so I switched gears. Which of my weaknesses could I exploit?

I don't always know when not to do something. But if I set my pride aside, maybe my socially-inappropriate ideas could be useful. After all, it was me getting out of abuse, not a popular cheerleader with all right social graces. How about if I started with my anger?

#123. ANGER

I'm angry that you can buy your way
Out of being a sex offender
Although I am not saying he did
Money for a good lawyer
Connections with the court

I'm angry that people in power
Do not understand the dynamics
Of middle-class abuse

I'm angry that people who could have helped
Didn't realize until
It was too late

I'm angry that I couldn't
Be clearer describing
Tragedy

I'm angry that being autistic
Made my attempts for help
Fall silent
Without the expressions
People expect

#124. UNCLEAR

I'm not even sure if any of it makes sense in words
There are no words for these levels of pain
Even "pain" is fatally indiscriminate

I liked thinking and playing with words
It was more fun when I was younger
Without crisis followed by crises

Trying to make sense of it for
People able to help
I can't even make sense of the pain
Instead
I want to reverse time
I want to play with icosahedrons
I want to like my mind
Again

Why can't I just
Have everyone evaporate from earth
And play
With figures of carbon as peers
Discussing the lights of reflection
C-60 and C-70
I know how to make them sparkle
Light waves can bounce
Easier than people

Talking to people
Trained to listen
I feel like dull pencil lead
Life withdrawn
Being used to shade in
Their drawings

I want to listen to music
Do anything
Be alive
But trying to explain
My life here with people
I think they might
Like it better if I was
Dead

Then they could
Extract the truth
I can't answer

Their questions
My heart presses
Forcing blood cider to drain

I can't force
Words
From my mouth when
The pressure on my heart
From life
Leaves a vacuum
Sucking all the images
Inside

#125. NO WORDS

It took me time to say
That every time
He lost a job
I knew
Becca would masturbate 'til she bled
Long before
A missed link caused
A pop-up
On an employer's screen

I couldn't say
That I felt guilty
For passing out in pain
That I couldn't remember

The details of him beating
Them

I'm sorry
I sat there and stared
When you asked
But I'm also
Not

Because
What you asked me to do
Was too much for me
Figure it out
Tell us
You are too damn
Demanding

I know you wanted
Relief from the turmoil
An explanation that completed
Your little form
And more importantly
Let you know how to help
But
It's not okay to ask a mother
To give you the details of abuse
In front of a child

It's not acceptable

To ask
Her
To speculate about what
Could have happened
When her heart
Won't let her
You played unfair

I know you wanted to help
I know you cared
But I refuse to draw a picture
When my heart
Is so pressed
That it can no longer
Bleed

#126. THE BENEFITS OF SCHOOL

There were many benefits to going back to school. I got a scholarship that covered my daughters going to preschool. I was able to enjoy learning and using my mind again. I had medical insurance. I had the chance to have my PTSD, migraines, and narcolepsy treated. I had something that did not make me feel like a failure. I had a place where questions were answerable.

#127. BEGGING GOD FOR A NEW CHALLENGE

God, now that I can think a bit again, would you help me find avenues to learn new things? I feel like the time that I used to spend just trying to make it through the abuse is now being used just to make it through all of the appointments in the path of healing, trying to answer the riddles of time and perspective.

It's not that I don't like doctors, counselors, occupational therapists, but sometimes those appointments just feel so consumed by their chatter. I am sure that I am probably just wanting to use thinking as an escape, but can I please have some time to look at ideas from 12 points of view or work on some geometric proofs?

It's great not to be as worn down, but all of this healing needs to be broken up, too. Any subject, other than mental health, child development, or medicine, would be fine. I don't care if you have me learn all the names of the parts in a car engine. I take that back. Let my brother have that one. I'd prefer something that speaks to the echo in my heart.

#128. DOCTORS TRY SO HARD

> Doctors try and read bodies: their color and pulse
> Taught to read a language simple as Morse code
> When a body was made to speak in symphonies
> With very precise tones
> I can't imagine trying to capture the sound with only
> The ways
> They know

#129. TURNOVER

> Mental health counselors
> And psychiatrists

Bring so much
Instability to their profession
Burning out
Moving on
Rarely do they last even a year

Ashley had three psychiatrists within
A year
The one she has now
Starting a new practice
But first
Standing in the doorway
Child in hand
He stopped me and said
"You are doing a good job.
It shows."
Layers of pain
He took off
In a moment

It cost him eight words
I was used
To being blamed
Judged
Told the kids
Needed something else
Which I translated
"Not me"
But a make-believe version

A mom with the
Superpower
Of escaping abuse
Unscathed

#130. IMAGES

God, how can I get the memories
Out of my mind
The thoughts of all the things
We experienced

It makes me think of
Pornography
How do You deal with
Those images
Sprawled out in front
Of our culture

The pain in peoples' eyes
The men as well as the women
How do you find a blanket
Large enough to cover it

#131. STORIES

The girls ask me for stories
But I have the hardest time

Thinking of them
Without remembering the crap, too

So I tell them about my brother
Putting spaghetti on his head
Taking me to a play
Tricking me into eating a pepper
Watching me guzzle his soda

Little does he know
He's the one
Who gets me through
I count on memories from him
To make me smile

The girls have heard the stories
A million times
But they are safe, with no
Strings attached

#132. MY REQUEST

When I was younger, I heard a camp story that explained the night sky. A blanket was stretched to cover the earth. The stars were holes that the birds had made with their beaks. I would like all my memories of the abuse to be covered by a blanket hung way up in the sky. Then, I could enjoy those moments that my children carved out as if they were stars in the night.

#133. APOLOGY

As part of his domestic violence therapy, Frank was required to write me an apology, but he refused to give it to me. He justified it by saying, "It would just make you mad." I always wondered about that. Mad because it was inconsistent? Mad because it contained things I didn't remember? Mad because he blamed me? Probably not, it was for treatment so, surely, they would not have let him get away with that, right?

According to the program director, Frank was doing well in therapy. He talked and participated. But I wondered, why does he get to control me not being mad or having a reaction?

I had never hit him. I didn't even yell or throw things. I got weak with strong emotions and could not throw or hit even if I wanted to. His issues with abuse were not about him being out of control of his response, but with him being in control and using that to control others with fear and intimidation. He was not a shouting, raging mess. He was calculated and guarded, just like he was with his missing apology.

#134. A MANTRA

> God, continue to bring life
> To my soul
> Keep breathing
> It's working

#135. CALMING DOWN

I got out some bubbles
A bowl, and a straw
And began blowing
Until ALL

My air is consumed

A mess
Refusing
The bounds of a brim

Overpouring
As it beckons
The girls' hearts
To join in

I am enjoying the ideas from the girls' occupational therapist. I like having concrete ways to help them settle a bit.

#136. NOMINATED

I had a teacher nominate me for an award at the university. Once nominated I had to turn in essays, complete an interview, and submit recommendations from some of my other professors. Between kids, their appointments (occupational & physical therapy, speech therapy, and counseling), studying, and keeping up with the housework, I didn't think there was a chance in hell that I would get the award.

I filled out the essays between being puked on and a kid wetting the bed. Needless to say, my life felt pretty raw. What was my biggest accomplishment in the last year? I assumed that they would have applicants talking about their great research project or how they organized some group to affect change. Figuring I had no chance of getting selected, I spoke my truth. My biggest accomplishment: I had not committed suicide. What made me proud? I helped a transfer student connect with some clubs so he didn't feel isolated.

#137. SELECTED

The surprise that followed my essays was one that shocked me. I had been selected to be interviewed. Out of the thousands of students, I was one of the "final 20." As I sometimes do when I can't sleep, I played around online until I found an email that the interviewers had circulated to each other. If one is persistent and creative a lot of things can be found, unencrypted. You'd be amazed.

I went into the interview figuring I would just tell them the truth. I had no investment in getting an award, but two questions in, I could not keep a straight face. I hid a laugh as the third interviewer presented his question. He looked at me puzzled. Certain that I would never be chosen, I told the panel why I could not keep it together. I had hacked into the email, found the list of questions, and was humored that they asked them word for word in order. To which one of them asked, "What is our next question?" I told them the next three, and they all relaxed.

Instead of following their script, they got to ask questions from their hearts. What was I planning on learning in my classes the upcoming year?

What had kept me in school despite all the challenges? At what point did I know I was invested? What surprised me the most?

I wasn't planning to learn a lot from the curriculum, as much as I was planning on learning from the other students. I loved hearing their perspectives, histories, and desires. The thing that kept me in school: PubMed and research databases. The minute I knew I was invested: when I took my entire welfare check to pay for tuition, not sure if I would get a scholarship or not to pay for the utilities. And my biggest surprise: at first I thought it was the fact that clip in colored highlights could be a big conversation starter. But then I remembered my first day studying in the Women's Center.

Upon walking into the building, I saw a guy staring at his computer and exclaiming "Oh my God, that cleavage is awesome. Someone could get lost between those breasts!" That was the opposite of what I was expecting. It turned out that it was a picture of himself dressed as a woman.

#138. PLAYING ONLINE

My ability to read and find things online helped me a few other times as well. A person can learn a lot if they search for patterns instead of just words. Plus, if one is creative enough, it is possible to get a lot of information, memos, and projects. Over the years, I have coined a new term: "breaking Google" to describe any search that yields only two or three meaningful results without any extra babble.

When I come across something that really should not be public, I tell the people responsible. One example was occurred when I typed a query of the five rarest mutations I could find in my raw data 23 and my results. This search brought up three people's data that was stored in a university genome project. The more precise I got, the more information came up. In the end, I emailed the database caretakers. It should not be possible to link peoples' full names, zip codes, and DNA and find the actual person out of everyone in the US since they had forgotten to check the file names for surnames. I admit, I did have to consult Facebook and marathon times, figuring people with rare diseases are often motivated to do what they can to find cures. It is true, a lot of people probably would not take time to study the participants' order in the database to find siblings who came in together, but I had to have an escape from my life to make something, anything, seem solvable.

Research for my brain is like movies for someone else; it relaxes me. I find it therapeutic, especially if it contains patterns. Patterns are my autistic, favorite subject.

#139. PRONE TO INFECTION

Broken down from the years of stress, I found myself especially vulnerable to infections, many of which were hard to treat. I got three HIV tests just to see if he had given me that in addition to the nightmares, but they were all negative.

I had cellulitis and pneumonia several times. One time sticks out in my memory. I had been in the hospital for close to a week. Five different IV antibiotics later, I was still ill. At one point, I became completely delirious. I could hear what was going on, but I started losing my grounding. The doctor requested a psych evaluation.

The social worker came and asked me lots of meaningless questions. When she asked me to spell "world" backward, all I could think was how much DELRIHW looked like delirium with spinning letters at the end. My mind felt like it was spinning and I just wanted her to shut up.

At the end of her evaluation, she asked, "Do you have any thoughts of hurting yourself or someone else?" I must admit that I did, but I said "No."

Do I want to hurt her?
Part of me does
I want her
To step back
And think
Maybe even
Understand
Empathize
If I could teach her
But
I would have to
Help her
Touch the pain
I am feeling
Would that be wrong
To want
A hospital social worker
To reflect
How I felt
To be autistic
A patient
Sick
Worn down
By talking
I'd like to
Grant her an autistic body

For an hour
I'd like to mess
With her schedule
And meals
I'd like to force
Her to answer a
Multitude
Of questions
Each with one correct, preset answer
As she experiences the pain
Of cellulitis
The burning of ice packs
Machines beeping and
Lights flickering
Thousands of times
Per solitary
Minute
So "Yes"
I'd want her to feel pain
My pain
So that she
Would be more sensitive
Is it wrong
To want to hurt her
Like that?

When she was done, she left without giving me another medicine. I wondered while they were asking the same questions each day, couldn't they ask questions that might make a difference? Questions like: As a society, is there a way for us to stop domestic and cultural violence? What is the best way for children who have witnessed abuse to heal? How can we rebuild the vitality of people whose lives have been torn apart? But laying there, those questions were too much to bear. Even a mind that is sharp and clear could not find an answer to those questions that day.

When she left, I went back to one of my trusted mysteries, a question posed to me in the second grade. How do you split a dollar four ways? The correct answer: four quarters. But if you think about it in a different way, you will discover that paper can never yield metal when it splits.

Delirium is a great caretaker for lines of symmetry and the physics of reflections induced by mirrors. Someday I will discover how to get the angles correct for eight images, four of both the front and back of the bill. For the time being, it was a nice distraction from the beeping machines, the smell of disinfectant, and pulling at my IV.

In school I had a friend tell me that I was the smartest dumb person she knew. She was probably right, but for now, my silly interpretation of a question still brought me entertainment and relief.

#140. CHANGING THE TRAJECTORY

I started off in engineering as a major, figuring I could at least provide financially for my kids. But half-way through, I realized that my kids didn't need a mom with lots of money as much as a mom who could help them as they recovered. My weaknesses were not in math and science; what I struggled with: The Humanities. I switched my major to something truly challenging for me. Don't laugh. I went into Liberal Studies. For all of the ignorant, liberal studies is a soft major, easy to complete. Not for me.

A secret? I still studied in the upper-class engineering room and helped with homework that people found hard.

But instead of fluid dynamics and linear algebra, I tried to understand people and they are a conundrum. The very things I asked God not to have me learn I had to learn. Theories and tests of my weakest areas. Getting an autistic, single mom to learn about social dynamics at a college level when said mom had given her best friend in high school deodorant for her birthday because she said she liked things that smelled good... That proved to be a hard task, but valuable.

#141. CHILD DEVELOPMENT

One of the classes I took was on child development. I knew a lot of the theories, reaching back to my childhood when my mother was a professor. I used to sit in the lecture halls, coloring or at least organizing my crayons in various ways.

There was a single sentence that opened my eyes regarding children. One of my classmates was blind. He told me in the hall, before class, that the teacher gave him a pass on the child observation project we all had to do because he couldn't see. That one comment revolutionized the way I "saw" my kids.

I could not read their faces and expressions. I was not gifted in knowing what would magically soothe them. I could not see it, but when I heard him say that he was excused because he couldn't see, I thought it was ridiculous. One does not have to see kids to observe their behavior and patterns. Even without sight, he could hear the child's movements and words. He could describe their interactions. His observation might not say the child had dirty blond hair, but he could describe the things that mattered.

Even without "seeing" my kids' facial expressions, I could use my other senses to see what they needed.

I made a list.

Without eyes, I can
Pay attention to their breathing
Watch their approach to other people
And symbolically to topics or ideas
I can tally their interest
In different activities
Observe what settles them
And what rallies their defenses
I can hear their voices
Listening for nuances
Differences with time or day

But unlike my friend, who was improperly labeled incompetent, I could see. I just had to learn how to interpret the data.

I might not naturally monitor the angles of their
Facial muscles or the openness of their eyes
Or whatever non-autistic people see
I might not know the difference between
Sunscreen in their eyes
Lack of sleep
Or a bad day at school
But I can see color

I could try and correlate
Colors of make-up
With them in different states
Tints of yellow or green

And try
To decipher
What they might need

I began
A lifelong quest
To understand
To be the mother
They always needed
I could dissect natural instinct
Untainted by autism or trauma
I might be late, but I was determined

It pissed me off
That one of the girl's psychiatrists said
I was emotionally unavailable

But in the end
My weakness
Added to a mother's will to fight
Forced my girls' strength
Identifying emotions
Self-governing
Emotional control

But not without a lot of trials
Observed by everyone
First

#142. WRONGLY DIVIDED

A boy attacked Ashley
On a field trip
Celebrating
The last day of school
Her class had gone
Swimming
That night
Was a party
To celebrate the day
But before
She told me
Two days later she showed me

Bruising by her vagina
Grab marks
Bruises of handprints dug into her arms
I called the abuse hotline
What do I do for
My child
She was attacked

The Emergency Room
A male police officer
Taking photos of her body
Naked
Did she fight back?

Yes, she scratched the attacker's chest

The officer visited his home
Spoke to the school
Ashley had not
Rushed to a teacher for help
She was quiet and downcast
Part of it must have been her fault

He calls
Tells me his conclusion
Wishes he had seen her before
The weekend with her dad
And speaks to her on the phone

Her fault she was attacked
My fault that he told her

His brashness and stupidity
Make me question
Is it my fault
I was abused
Because my words could have hurt Frank
Because I finally responded

Not rational
But pain
Speaking
Critiquing the growth

I had just
Discovered

#143. TOTALLY CONFUSED

That summer, I followed his logic all the way to a mental breakdown. Ashley wanted to be baptized and the church wanted the whole family to attend. I remember looking at her and deciding that life was not worth living if it meant we had to play the perfect, intact family again.

I cannot live and accept these conditions
I cannot reconcile the pressure of others
to fit in, hold a standard, and pretend.
I'd rather be dead.

After the service
My brain snapped
It broke with the strain
Of reality breaking in
I didn't kill myself

But I thought
I must be dead
I felt like
I had
Eaten carbon emissions
Or methane

My world spinning

A fairy tale nightmare
Of sorts
My parents caught
The girls
While I floated down
From insanity

I could not play
Wife to that man
Again

#144. NOTE TO SELF

Don't ever say
That a social worker is
A government spy
Even if:
It's the third time she's asked you
In a week
If you know who she is, and
You are exhausted
Drained and fatigued
You just want to sleep
Have her stop talking
To you
Plus, you just
Feel like being
A brat

Even if you know
Her notes are being used
To defend expenses to
Government-funded
Insurance

Ordinary people stop conversations
When you say something
True in spirit, but ridiculous in life
Mental health people
They just don't know when to let sick people
REST
And they don't get autistic jokes

I think they
Should be required
To take a class
"Building A Competent Memory"
They can't even remember
Where they work
Or why

Any protocol that keeps me up past nine
Is annoying

God, I don't care if you have to flash images
Of Reagan in my mind
Remind me: Just say "NO" to social workers
They seem to like that answer

One of the things that people sometimes misunderstand about autistics is that we have to write a mental procedure manual for social interactions. For years, mine included the following:

> Proper answer to a question posed by a social worker: "No."
> Proper answer to a question posed by a doctor: "Two or three."
> Proper answer to a question posed by a police officer:
> "I don't know."
> Proper answer to a psychiatrist: (Just stay silent); any profession that dares say they understand the workings of the human mind is good at filling in the blanks.

If you ever get bored when talking to a well-meaning health interrogator, imagine using my answers. If you tell them the proper answer enough times in a row, you'll see that they work.

Although, now that my protocol is known, my counselor alerted my doctor. "Never believe her if she says 'two or three,' she loves numbers and will never use a range." Regardless, different professions do write questions favoring specific replies.

#145. UNAVAILABLE

Healing from abuse is a lot like driving down a gravel road. Occasionally, a rock will fly up and hit you in the face.

Somewhere along the line, I realized that a psychiatrist had included, in Ashley's diagnosis, that I was emotionally unavailable. That baffled me. In her judgment, the sociological factor most impacting Ashley's impulsivity was me, and that was before I learned to just be silent.

Why was I labeled unavailable? Because I had four kids and was tired? Because I was separated from my abuser and trying to recover from head injuries? Because I had autism and didn't have the facial expressiveness of the non-autistic? Or maybe because I said during the interview, "I have cataplexy which limits my ability to show emotions when I am extremely stressed"? Or perhaps the real reason was she chose to interview Frank and me in the same room, together, even when she knew there was a history of domestic violence. That was fucked up.

Separating from an abusive person, trying to provide safety, having friends who could take her to school, and being willing to go to the damn hospital with MY abuser. I was working hard to be WHOLE, WELL, and AVAILABLE. Plus, I was working hard to just ANSWER her questions.

Even though it happened years before, the anger and indignation hit a bit later when things were calmer. Insults have a way of doing that, and I was insulted. I went on a tirade:

"Do you know the problem with Christians? God is an emotionally unavailable parent. For that matter, do you know the problem with Jews, Muslims, Buddhist, Atheists, and EVERYONE on Earth? God is emotionally absent; except maybe Atheists have some other dilemma. Even the Bible states, God turned His face from Jesus on the cross. The very moment His Son needed Him. I'm being sarcastic, if you couldn't figure it out. Sometimes I sarcasm stupidly. It can be a verb, right?"

"Ashley's problem wasn't that I was emotionally unavailable. It was in her favor that I was emotionally battling to get free from Frank. Each human only has so much availability and getting free from domestic violence is taxing, just like raising a Son from the dead. Look at the fruit afterward. It was a plan that worked. I am certain that Jesus preferred to have God turn His face for a moment than be left on that damn cross."

Elsie told me to refrain from sarcasm, because I speak it with a straight face and it's scary not to know if I am serious. But for the rest of you, you might just have to figure it out on your own; and if you are a psychiatrist you will have to let me know if you really want my unfiltered, autistic ramblings or just time to sit in silence.

#146. FRANK'S NEW GIRLFRIENDS

Frank met a new woman within a few weeks of our divorce. I'm sure he knew her for longer than that. One day she called me, Frank had given her my number. She said she felt conflicted and wasn't sure if it was smart to marry a felon.

She repeatedly asked me about my relationship with him. I felt numb even trying to go back to those moments when we were together. I just told her, "It's important to listen to your heart. I can't answer that for you." Frank blamed me for ruining their relationship, but the truth is he had done that all by himself.

The next summer, Frank found a woman to marry. He was set ready to begin the idyllic journey of meeting his needs. They met over the internet, but this time he did not give her my number. They married a few months later. He insisted the girls be part of his wedding, even though one of them had never even met the lady.

#147. DISTRACTION

I spent the day answering questions online. I am one of the top contributors (and have gotten lots of "best answers") in physics, calculus, men's health, and self-harm? Kind of ironic considering I am not a man and don't cut or hurt myself. The physics and geometry I get. Although, I have been through a lot of hell. I think I just need to feel like I still make a difference in society. I need to do something to feel like I matter outside the walls of my home. Plus, there has to be some value in the internet other than dating felons.

#148. REGRET

When the abuse went to court, Frank's attorney argued the charge to a felony, coercion. I could never make sense that, but I also knew I couldn't testify. I could not feel that level of emotion and still have my jaw work. As society has changed and BDSM has come to the forefront, I have wondered why Frank didn't just find someone into being beaten and raped, if that exists. I was not coerced to be beaten and raped.

Coerced to write a letter: Yes.

Coerced to be someone's property: No.

#149. LITTLE THINGS

The phlebotomist at the lab makes flowers and animals with the tape after she takes the girls' blood. She goes above and beyond the requirements of her job, adding some joy. The girls call her "Rebecca the Great."

It's a pain that stress and injuries caused their thyroid levels to teeter up and down for a few years, but it is great to see people who can make even the unpleasant things seem a little fun.

#150. WITHOUT AN ANSWER

I had a wise friend ask
"What do you do when you are
in the middle of the ocean
with no land in sight?"
At first, I thought swim.
"To what?" his reply
With no answer, he prompted
"Sometimes, you need to tread water
Relax
Keep your chin up
And calm the demands
Of your heart"
Balancing them
With your lungs

There have been many times that his advice steadied me. I had to remember to keep my head up, reserve my strength, and focus on something that brings peace (not sharks and monsters under the water). His words reassured me.

#151. BROKEN

Some say
There is a void
That only God can fill
If I am a vessel like that

I'd want to be cracked
I'd want ALL the liquid
To fall out

Empty
In the presence of an
All present God
That's insane

#152. INSIGHT

Ashley told me something interesting today, "The most important thing to do when you are depressed is choose not to do things that make you depressed."

She is wise for a preteen. Don't be mean to myself. Don't call myself names. Don't do things that make me feel worse.

Her insight forces me to consider what triggers my depression and helps me remember not to punish myself by doing things that make me feel crappy.

#153. REDIRECT

Christy got into the habit of lashing out and hitting people. I tried putting her in time out, but she would sit on her bed and bite herself or hit her head into the wall behind her. I felt at a loss of what to do, so I made something up. I got her a punching bag. Her new "punishment" for hitting: do 15 push-ups and hit the bag until she was tired. After a while, she was going to the bag BEFORE she hit someone. She is just so angry, and rightfully so.

#154. SHAKEY

It is a process to learn

How to feel

Insecure

Unstable

Unsure

Inadequate

And still make

Good decisions

Still give life

Time

To change

#155. PERSISTENCE

An answer that can be written in a fortune cookie

Will never compare to one obtained with true discipline

Uncomfortably

In prayer

#156. WEAK

The doctors didn't seem to have any idea more than me on what was caus-ing the weakness that affected our breathing. Cataplexy should not be able to do that; it can cause weakness, but it does not affect the lungs.

My girls were still getting weak. They choked trying to swallow water. So, as any good mom would do, I used my unique skills to try and find a solution. The problem was my skills were off the charts weird. Just to give you an idea of the messes I got into, I discovered firsthand the dangers of searching online.

I am not talking about the anxiety of reading up on something and pan-icking about some mysterious disease (or more likely meeting a convicted felon). I am talking about situations like accidentally pulling up a bunch of encrypted emails from the Security Exchange Commission.

When that happened, and it has happened more than once, I have just said "oh shit, oh shit," backspace, backspace, and tried to get out of the mess. Google has always been my friend for searches, but I have a habit of searching for patterns, not just topics.

This time was different, I had searched for a topic, "MHY7 q1334*"; I guess that was the first part of the SEC email lines that particular day, or some phrase that was repeated in emails the same location. Or maybe, the Security Exchange Commission is conducting clandestine research regard-ing genetic mutations. I don't think so. Regardless, be careful online (and if you are the SEC, please, please, PLEASE improve your encryption so you can stop messing up my searches).

#157. NURTURING CHILDHOOD

We found an intelligent dentist. He asked Elsie to open her mouth like a lion. It was so much better than asking her about boyfriends at the age of four, like her previous dentist. It feels good to be able to surround my kids with people who are not obsessed with sex and weirdness.

#158. A DREAM

Once again
You ask
What do I remember
But this time
It's not as close
In the span of time
What do I remember
Of You
I had a dream of You
Today
Centuries ago
Sitting in a meadow

Just the thought of You
All those years back
Embracing my humanity
Loving me
Breathing visions of stars
Into my soul

You truly played
A song that I can hear
Even now
Nothing could hold it
Through deaths
Tragedy
Wars
And lost sons
Your music continues

#159. FOLLOWED BY ANOTHER DREAM

I had a dream
Of Ravens
My friend Lillie
Transformed
Able to cleanse even death
From the darkness of night
They emerge
Unafraid
Carrying something
Light
As if greeting the sun

They travel to places
Uncomfortable
And hidden
Guardians of life

Scrapping away
The secrets
Harboring little beads
Or trinkets
A strand of ribbon

Their curiosity
Pulling the useful
So it doesn't get lost
But donned
Worthy of flight

The gifts they bring
As presents
To people deemed worthy

The raven of dreams
Dared to see
The value of
Words

Like sparkly metal
And beads
To collect over time
And free

Each flight
A night
One item alone

Gathered
To bring
Through the darkness
The secrets
Held and embraced by time
Tomorrow they utter
A gift to appear

Cras'ing even in Latin

#160. TUCKED IN WITH A STORY

God, it was the ancient Vedic astrology that helped me first make sense of what had happened. To embrace what my life had become.

A story
A grace
Written in stars
You authored
A story
No book could contain
It had to be held
By the sky

When I look up at night, I hear You singing Your love in their movements. You say goodnight in the sweetest of ways.

#161. BEDMATES

The girls mentioned that they laid in bed with Frank's new wife and him. I am not sure if the woman realizes the dangers that entails.

Even though I try to distract myself with adoration and academics, I keep returning to a deeper problem. A problem that defies a solution. A problem that I use the academics, and God's love, to break up.

#162. PRESSURE

My daughter came home and said that her dad
Would not stop talking
Prostitution
At her 13th birthday
She would not say any more
God, it's too painful to talk about

#163. FRIENDLY ADVICE

A sixth of an hour
God, I don't want to talk
To You anymore
I am mad at You. I am mad
That Your people are so rude

Just pray about it.
God has a plan,
They say

Can You hear the sarcasm

Dripping off my mouth? I'd like to take them

Tie them by their toes, and hang them

Upside down

Until some blood can reach their hearts

And brains

Remember the saying

If You don't have anything nice

To say

Don't say anything at all

Well, I'd like to change it to:

Just shut up

Shut up already

Your kids talk too much

They think they are being nice

But there are some pains

That don't

Respond to words. Some situations

That don't

Need encouragement

The only thing to do

Be here

Just sit with me

Let me cry

Not make sense

Let me muster enough strength

To get through
Another
Ten minutes

One breath
One heartbeat
At a time

#164. TEARS

I was in the violence
For far too long
And when I was quiet
I was too quiet, almost
Dead
No wonder my children
Shout and climb
And pull and tear
As they grasp in a panic
Frantically
Spotting the rips
In the fabric
Me
But this too
Can be mended
I will stitch it
They'll see
Again and again
And again, if need be

Even if

My thread must fight

Artfully arching in all the light

Weaving a fabric

Replacing the old

Overlapping, outpacing

Consuming the hole

Making fabric that's sturdy

And steady

And bright

Fabric to hold them

In the silence of night

#165. HEALING

People say, "Just trust God to heal you" not to comfort, but to say, "Silence your pain." God does heal, but healing is gross. People cough up phlegm as they recover from pneumonia. They shed sticky, crusty scabs as they recover from a fall. Is it possible that my pain, my indignation, and my anger are all part of healing? A false appearance of wellness is not.

Even when a wound heals, it can leave a scar. It leaves a reminder of what was there and what happened. In the right place, a scar like that is solely cosmetic. In another location, a scar has the capacity to restrict function. I think too many people believe they are commenting on tough, restrictive scars when they are prematurely ripping off scabs and prolonging the time spent healing. My prayer is that abuse victims will be able to symbolically vomit, scab up, and look like shit but recover. Healing from violence sucks, and it should take a while.

#166. FINDING COMFORT

Can I just watch crime shows
And pretend
The actors are being kind to me
Instead of the victims
In the show?

Part of my problem is that
It hurts too much to have
Real people respond
So can I just pretend?

I appreciate the screenwriters
Showing me
That my experience is not unique
That it could be worse
That there are people who understand
Can I pretend You are those people
Listening, protecting
Me

#167. SOCIOPATHS ON TV

There is something wrong with
Most dramatic TV crime shows
The sociopaths all have tells
They act differently

Their sentence structure
Revealing their pathology

In real life, they don't
Their only tell
The overwhelming ability to make people
Trust them

They don't stand out
Except, as people who have life together
On TV actors must act like
Sociopaths
The narratives tell the truth
But the videos
Filled with lies

If I had to write a script
Of a sociopath's life
I would not tell the actor
Until after all
The community scenes
Were shot

I'd just tell them that
They are smart, witty,
And kind
They have a great life
Deeply respected and valued
Let them revel in pride

I don't know an actor
Who could really
Delight in pain
And keep it together
Just playing that part
Would have to hurt someone
To the depths of their soul

#168. A SOCIOPATH'S TELLS

Confidence
Treating people like toys
Baiting people to catch them
Too smart as a game
Showing off their esteem
Batting authority to
Delight in pain
Discomfort, unease
Keeping their prey
Teetering
As they own the day

#169. RECIPROCITY

I threw his phone into the yard
It broke into pieces
I have always felt proud of that

Not that a phone was
Equivalent to years of abuse
But I did something

Sometimes I feel guilty
That I feel proud
About being mean
But I think there is a deeper level
He put his phone back together
And it worked
I think, karmically, maybe I
Can put my daughters and me
Back together, too

My job is taking longer
But hey
I have always been good at puzzles

#170. PHONE VOICE

Have you ever listened to someone speak on the phone? Someone called us today. Elsie answered and the person calling thought she was me! God, I want to be like that. I want someone to hear me and think I sound like You. I think that would be funny. Families do have dialects. The cool thing about Yours, it can be spoken in ALL the languages.

#171. UNCERTAINTY

There were so many situations I didn't know how to sort out or handle. I found myself writing in an attempt to pull out the answers from the crevices of my heart.

#172. WISDOM

The worse a situation is
The more you need to
Shut up
And listen
To your heart

Filter your thoughts
Through
The wisdom of
Your elders
But not their actual words

Their knowledge of words
Will always be
Fumbled
But their spirit
holds the answer
you'll need

God, I have a question. Have You ever died? I'm not asking theoretically, as in was Jesus on the cross. I mean have You ever been so exhausted that time stopped existing, matter stopped existing? Sometimes I feel so depleted that I don't know if I will have the energy to respond. Has that happened to You? How did You find the presence of mind to manage to start again? Was it like the big bang? Did You just condense and retract until all the matter in the universe was bound together? Does time slow to a stop in that type of situation?

It seems like it should. Do I even need to consider it? Sometimes I think of Einstein or contemplate Feynman's Lectures on Physics. I imagine Einstein playing the violin and meditating on the connections between time, space, vibrating strings, and imposed fractions. That's what I think about when I play my viola. There are so many problems that can be explored with a stringed instrument. I've played now for 25 years; I still sound awful, but I love seeing the connections.

There is a type of safety in the conservation of energy and matter. It takes away the fear of not existing. No matter how worn I am, there is potential in death.

#173. FOR HEAVEN'S SAKE

A stranger asked Christy for nude pictures online. Even without their dad, there are so many predators. It's sick.

#174. CHILDREN'S PAIN

God, You know that a B flat sounds different depending on the relationship in space and time between the instrument and the listener, right? I am not sure if being omnipresent prevents You from experiencing that. Regardless, is that why notes sound different when I play my viola and the sound vibrates through my jaw?

Does it mute or alter the noise to hear my pain when we touch? Does my daughters' pain sound different when You hear it through my ears instead of by Yourself? Does my role as their parent alter the sound like light getting refracted as it passes through the surface of water?

#175. EARPHONES

I've started putting in earphones and placing my phone in my apron. It's not even playing anything, but the girls don't know that. It's nice just to give them a visual cue. There are a lot of things they can do on their own, it just reminds them and saves me from having to speak.

#176. TO DO LIST

    Get groceries
    Call the school
    Take out trash
    Wash dishes
    Laundry
    Get over trauma
    Answer questions
    Pay bills

    Get a shower
    Describe the past

Have some flashbacks

Want to give up

Acknowledge the pain

Rewire the lawn mower

Try not to flee

Basically

Be a mom

And grieve

#177. A SCHOLARSHIP

I got a scholarship from a pharmaceutical company, despite switching my major to Liberal Studies. I don't see myself working for them in the future, but I do try to throw in my two cents when I run across one of their projects, especially if they are forgetting the chemical sensing TRP nerves when trying novel ways to treat pain. My mind has healed faster than my body, I think. I'm sure going back to school has helped a bit, too.

When I think of all I have learned, I ponder what would have been lost if I had not gotten divorced. What if I was still being beaten for scratching dry skin instead of standing up naked for my husband after a shower? I realize that it might take a while before all the kinks of abuse get worked out, but the tragedy that was avoided by divorcing makes it worth it. At some point, the balance between my mental and physical health should be restored, too, or so I can hope.

By the way, Elsie put pennies between every key in our old worn out piano. I've had several people look at it. I think I am going to have to find someone to rip it apart and burn it for wood. She was trying to put in "quarters" to see if it could play songs like the music (box she saw on TV.

There is no way to play it now. Kids get the damn'dest ideas from the television.

Becca managed to switch the screen on my laptop 90 degrees. I took it to the university computer support and had four computer nerds try to figure out how to fix it. It took them two hours. Life with young children, when you think you know what your day will be like, you can be certain that you've got it all wrong.

I asked her to switch it back, but she didn't want to. The way she changed it, she could sit beside me and read the screen. This was before the function was included as part of standard programming. Rewriting the axes of a computer is not something most four-year-olds could do. But Becca, she was terrifyingly smart. Later on, she had some head injuries that brought her back into the above-average genius level.

Ashley was convinced by some of the girls at school that the way to make friends was to put super glue on a toilet in the girls' bathroom. There is genius, and there is absolute gullibility. Ashley is an avid reader, but she can find all sorts of practical ways to make my life more interesting all on her own.

Ashley also wrote notes to all of her classmates inviting them to a party at our house. She was kind enough to leave my number for people to RSVP. I came home, after my classes, to eight RSVP confirmations. I managed to answer the phone when the ninth parent called. "Just wanted to make sure this is a real party? The invitation looks like a kid made it."

I made Ashley call everyone and uninvite them. While it was sweet to add my phone number, I let her know I had to approve parties beforehand. No raves at my house, thank you very much. Her excuse, her sisters helped her write the invitations.

Not to be left out, Christy jammed an entire roll of toilet paper down the bathroom sink so we would not lose any water. I am making her an "experiment table" for the back yard, so we can try and contain her chemistry-is-the-coolest-thing-ever phase. We have all sorts of potions that she has made.

And for round two of children vs. Mom. It has been a tough week.

Rebecca thought it would be cool to draw spirals on the ceiling of her room with a permanent marker. She has apparently gotten into spiral addition problems and said her drawings help her think at night. I can relate to that. She is excited to start school.

Christy felt sad for the bugs in the heating vents, so she started secretly feeding them dried fruit in addition to the cereal. I also thought her medicine wasn't working; turns out she has been hiding it in the Kleenex box that is on the dining room table.

But Ashley earns the award as the culprit of the week. I thought she was organizing her sisters for a fun day in the sprinkler. They were getting wet, but she had planned all sorts of fun events for all of them as well. Scissors for grass cutting, which turned into haircutting on the side of the house. A sign to wave down every college boy that drove by to "come to a party." It only takes five minutes for that kid! She totally confused some frat boys, driving by to see a bunch of girls in bathing suits jumping up and down, come on, it's a fun party! The oldest of the girls were still attending elementary school. Good God, what have I gotten into having her as my first born? Oh, don't tell me. Some answers are frightening enough to spread over a lifetime. I love her.

Just breathe.

Elsie this week was perfect, but I got in trouble for bringing green frosting instead of white to her preschool gingerbread decorating event. Apparently, even in a place that rarely sees snow, it is a parental failure to bring grass colored frosting. The teacher made it very clear that I was not a contributing member to parent-child day. For what it's worth, the color did not concern the kids and other parents. I swear if that is the biggest thing for the teacher to be upset with, more power to her, she obviously has it a lot more together than me.

Elsie's doctor found a popcorn kernel in Elsie's at the yearly check-up. Ashley put it there. Seriously?!? I do not understand these girls. What inspires Ashley to come up with these ideas?

Ashley also convinced Christy to snort cat food. The pediatrician's advice line told me that I should take her to the emergency room so she could have her nose vacuumed out. I'm starting to think I should schedule time in my planner for her detours of excitement.

#178. MAKING ROOM

There are stations
Around our home
Like eddies in a river
Puzzles
Games
A trapeze
Places to cuddle
With large comfortable blankets
Comics to read
Giant hammocks and swings
I'd rather have my home filled
With safe little breaks
Than condemn my children
To a life and bored
Tied down by flashbacks
With no reprieve

#179. UNIQUE

Each of my girls
Has unique talents
Strengths learned
And developed
Without imitation
If only I could see into
The future

Ashley, a voracious reader,
Revels in Greek myths
Historical fiction
Fantasy

Rebecca, a mentor,
Leads thousands
Past depression, self-harm, despair
And learns with ease

Christy is a leader and builder
Whether houses
Zip lines with Legos
She is a designer
And she's amazingly
Graceful on a trapeze

Elsie is sensitive and sweet

Mastering the art

Of connection

She is so kind

To people, animals, and me

Plus, she is a teacher

#180. A DOSE OF HUMOR

I ordered a used food journal online. The one I got turned out to be partially filled in by a professional food critic in Hawaii. The girls and I spent a night reading the notes that he used to write articles. He would not eat until the afternoon, and then he would feel blindsided by how much he ate at dinner. I am coming to realize that these simple moments of laughter and community are crucial. Whether it is a puzzle that we do on the dining room table or a book of humorous situations, unguarded joy is important.

I am learning that movies on the computer are not optional for my family. It is good for the girls to have a distraction from the memories, a way of escape. I often wonder if one of the challenges to giving up smoking is learning to take breaks to rest and restore. Just like people need to get up and walk around the room occasionally, they need to be empowered to silence their mind and disengage from the harder subjects.

I do not think that Ashley needs more ways to zone out. I need a way to get her more present, but every time she experiences anything that reminds her of her dad, she freaks out. Simple techniques don't always suffice when there has been trauma.

#181. IMPULSIVITY

Head injuries are nasty little creatures
Twisting up a kid's soul
And robbing the mind
Becca today had a whole gang
Push against her

With villains such listed:
    Tetherball
    Playground bar
    Basketball
    Metal slide
    Sister's head
    Kitchen table
    Joining forces

The effects:
    Impulsivity
    A seizure
    Chalking "fuck"
    On the playground
    Slurring words
    Blurring vision
    Nausea
    Drop in skills
    Never reading
    Toys abandoned

And that
Doesn't even consider
Her early youth
It's obscene

#182. DOCTORS, UGHHH

I'm pissed at doctors today
Doctors should
Be forced to go to a foreign country
With a kid
And see a doctor who does not
Speak a single word of the same language
That's how it feels
To take my child to a doctor

Words that "seem simple"
But too vague
For an autistic brain
Then knowing the kid
Needs to be seen
And not being able to do anything
That doctors should do
Learn that language oneself
To be told
You just like to speak our language
You like our hospitality

My kids are weak!
I thicken liquids
So they don't cough it out
Sometimes they are gray
And all they can do
Is lay down on the couch
With low spO2

I hate your languages
Vagueness and theory
Hell, be human at least
But maybe you are
Maybe it's me
I just speak autistic

The truth
Oh people, who swear they have empathy
Taking a kid to your office
With all your sensory crap
Flickering lights, alcohol stench
It would be like you
Sitting on a griddle
Being mimicked
While you cry
Inside
The kid sitting next to you
Still needs a doctor
But no one
Can speak

The language of body

I'm pissed
Can't you see
I'm muted
But still a parent

#183. ELSIE

Elsie's been getting migraines
Puking until she falls asleep
On the floor
She doesn't want comfort
She still goes to school
But it hurts to see
Her laying in the bathroom

#184. HOW TO RESPOND

When a kid freaks out
There are many things
One can try
    Distraction
    Changing the surroundings
    Something soothing
    Fidgets
    Compression
    Never ending counseling appointments

Hours of occupational therapy

Long, boring lectures

Humor

Frustration

~~Death~~, oops, void that

Church

~~Drugs~~, never mind

Prayer

I just need ONE

That might actually work

Make that

FOUR

No, FIVE

(I'm impatiently waiting)

God, someday

Will You trust me

With a cheat sheet

I'm freaking out

Like my children and

I need You, HERE

#185. FIGHTING FIRE

Under Frank's hand, my girls didn't learn to defend themselves or take a stand. I let them practice. I just give it back. I learned the following approach when I was little. My family lived by some farmers who would burn their fields once a year to keep down the weeds and yield fruitful crops.

Yelling

Is not always bad

It is good

To see a kid

Once broken

Try it on like a garment

I just yell back

A few tones down

Not mad

Just engaged

Enough to reassure them

I won't leave them

In their anger

Giving them time to

Develop the skill

You can be angry

And safe

Controlled in your response

Not hijacked by pain

Or hurting others

It's an act I call

Fighting fire with fire

#186. STANDARD FOR SEX OFFENDERS

Frank took a screening for sex offenders. It showed he was attracted to prepubescent girls, ones the age of our daughters. The psychologist who did the test said it was understandable. A lot of men who look at pornography these days are attracted to young girls because that is what pornography depicts.

I think he must have gotten to her, too. How could someone, who knew a man admitted to beating and raping his wife hundreds of times, believe it to be inconsequential when that same man shows attraction to sexual images of children? Especially, considering he sees girls that very age every month overnight.

#187. GUILT

People ask if I feel guilty for not knowing that Frank would be an abuser before I married. But even the people, trained to see it, have gotten fooled. How would I be able to do something that trained professionals trained could not do? I don't feel guilty. A bit mad, yes. I am unsure of their reason behind the question.

#188. MY PART

> I wonder if my actions
> Showing kindness to Frank
> The cards
> The things I said in public
> Were valued at a dollar
> I don't know how much
> Would have been
> Payment for protection

At least some
Was for me
Wanting to believe
Everything would be okay
Not from fear of
Offending his ego
But me
Craving denial
Wishing I could
Be granted the truth
Of my lie

I've concluded: whether I was doing the nice things to feel safe or to stay in denial doesn't matter. I was wrong, but don't deserve to be blamed. Abuse of power confuses fault. What is important moving forward? I need to know danger should never be placated or indulged with denial.

#189. PORN

I typed in porn
And the images:
Big boobs
Hard cocks
Wide hips
Not women
Who look
Like girls
Before puberty

#190. BALANCING

How do I balance my fears
With the limited knowledge I have?
How do I listen to my children
While drawing myself back
In hopes that they are not true?
How do I evaluate the signals and effects
When I have no definite proof?

#191. SUPPORT

Facing the memories
Can't be done alone
When too overwhelmed
I need people to help
Or
I could drown in myself

My schedule must hold
Activities and interests
To balance the pull
Introspection too weighty

Mindless events
Or TV
So I don't just get focused
On pain

It's almost certain
To convolute my mind
Without people
To share with

As I grapple with nightmares
Flashbacks
And triggers
And the words
Of my children

#192. MY RESPONSE

I would rather be able to woo
Someone's heart
With kindness and words
Than command a body
With sexual spreads

I know the value
Of covering
Another's weakness

What could possibly be obtained
By pornography
With pictures of girls
That's sick

But the reality of life is that some people do find pleasure from that, and the rest of us must do whatever we can to protect the fragileness of youth.

#193. A WEEKEND EACH MONTH

For about a year and a half, my girls had been staying with their father one weekend a month and two weeks at Christmas. They usually stayed at a hotel, went swimming, and showered. But the older girls told me that they can no longer stay with him. Ashley told me it isn't safe for her sisters.

But if I didn't send them, I could be charged, blamed for impeding his time with them. For a while, I had family or friends take the girls to a fast food place to be transferred to him. Slowly, people have started refusing, saying they are uncomfortable even being part of a transfer.

Unsure of my options, I met with a lawyer. She sent Frank a letter stating the girls were unwilling to meet with him if it wasn't supervised. He chose to agree as long as it didn't go to trial, as long as the girls didn't say why in court.

The whole thing is screwed up, but at least the girls will be safer now.

#194. SUPERVISED VISITS

The staff at the center are awesome. It is nice to work with people who understand how sociopaths work. I don't have to do much; they get it.

The girls are now able to say if they want to see him or not. They can log it. Now there is no question if I am refusing to take them or not. I am protected from being blamed.

There are separate parking lots for each parent. I don't have to see Frank at all. The best thing, however, is the girls get to choose. They are finally empowered to decide if it is safe for them to see him.

#195. MANIPULATION

Frank thought he would try to tangle the girls' emotions, but the staff cut the appointment short. The girls came out ashen. The staff spoke with each one, gave them a blanket and let them curl up as they told me what happened in another room. That night, the girls wore those blankets home. They held them so tightly; I don't think they will let them go anytime soon.

While I am not glad he was able to sneak in some abuse, I am thankful that the staff was there when it happened.

#196. STAIRS

Becca and Elsie bonked heads as they collided on the stairs. Elsie seems fine, but all of Becca's other head injuries appear to be synergistically opposed to a quick recovery.

#197. DOWN HILL

Rebecca is having a hard time with migraines. She is nauseous a lot and doesn't want to eat. I am trying to help her rest. She throws up when she looks at a screen and has stopped wanting to do things she previously enjoyed, namely puzzles and reading.

#198. ALONE

I will leave you alone when
You can be alone safely
Until then
I'll wish I had time
And space
And resources
To be
Alone

#199. BINGING OR STARVING

Becca is depressed; she stopped eating. It isn't being thin that motivates her, she just wants to die.

Becca
Won't eat
Since she hit
Her head
She lives on ice

Her doctor
Switched her to
Ice cream
We'll see
She's losing her
Vitality

Ashley started binging, dissociatively eating to hold down all that she feels. How should I feed four girls each with their own issue? I have one binging in the middle of night. Another whose stress irritates her to the point that she is only willing to eat ice (and now ice cream). A third whose medication limits her appetite. And a fourth who just eats like a kid.

I can put out healthy food for every meal. And wait. Trust, and deal with the mental health first. I feel like my family is a tangled knot that I have been elected to figure out.

> Why my dear child
> In the middle of night
> Do you rise and devour
> All that's in sight
>
> What is the pain
> That consumes you
> With darkness and shame
> That binds you
> With hunger
> That will not
> Stop

I knew one thing for certain, I could not let food become a power struggle. With the history my family has, that would ensure a permanent eating disorder.

#200. DINNER

Everyone ate turkey sandwiches and mandarin oranges for dinner. That's it. It was refreshing.

#201. WHITE NOISE MACHINE

It was a challenge to manage the girls' issues and responses and still honor my individual recovery. Slowly, I turned to writing in an attempt to pour out my emotions and memories. The next few paragraphs were birthed in that manner. I found them creviced in the binding of First John.

"I don't know how to separate his touch from my skin, how to peel the pain away. I've tried with children. They came, they grew. They passed the gate. But his touch has remained. He said I needed to be chastised. He tried to control love. Do this. Do that. Or I will beat you. Rape you. Bring you to touch me. I'll force your love, but he couldn't. He said that I wanted it and needed it, but I could never want that."

His words had the power to echo.

"God, can You make a white noise machine just for me? One that I can put on my belly and watch how it balances his nasty speech? I know if You can make all the birds, with their various songs, You can do that one for me. I don't want to wait. Make a white noise machine, even if that machine must be made from all the beauty of the sights and the sounds of the whole world that I see. Let it bombard me until all that interference dies out."

#202. PARENTING

There is a man in the Bible

With four prophetic girls

Everyone says

He's blessed

But I wonder

I think God

Comes into a life

And speaks to children

Because some kids

Are just too much

To raise with human words

#203. STRAIN

"Ashley is being stalked at school. The boy said he will commit suicide if she doesn't go out with him. He follows her home. Sends notes through friends. She's freaked. Even without the history of abuse, rape, and craziness, it'd be scary. I spoke to the school. It hasn't stopped, but summer break is coming and I hope the situation will die out."

The break came and went. Time had not helped. My heart ached for Ashley, but also for the boy. He needed help, too.

I took Ashley to her doctor who adjusted Ashley's medication in an attempt to reign in my daughter's anxiety. Ashley reacted, violently.

Then everyone was scared. Ashley seemed to be losing track of time and memory when she acted out. It reminded me of her dad in a way. It reminded her sisters, too.

#204. COURT

The issue with the boy ended up in court. A judge issued a restraining order. I went to the county health department and got Ashley (and her sisters) on the wait list for counselling. The mental health services in our town were excessively strained, just like the people they served. It took a while to get help.

#205. ESCALATION

When December came, I still had not heard from Behavioral Health, i.e. counseling services. A third of the way through the month, they called. Intakes would be in February.

Ashley's breaking point did not wait until February. It happened a week later, in December, when she found a letter from the boy in her backpack. When she found it, she ran down the stairs in an attempt to get as far from the letter as she could. The boy was no longer attending the same school and she was terrified that he managed to get a letter in her backpack despite the order that he could not use peers to pass messages.

Unfortunately for us, Christy was going up the stairs at the time when Ashley ran down. Ashley pushed her out of the way as she fled. That sent Christy cascading down the stairs. As you can imagine, being pushed down the stairs did nothing to help Christy feel safe. On the contrary, it triggered her trauma and shook her sense of safety to her core.

The situation was simply too much for our family.

#206. WHAT HAPPENED NEXT

Ashley, who was already on high alert, went emotionally flat. She wandered outside in below freezing weather unaware of the cold, falling asleep without even a sweater. She just looked vacant. There was only a little bit of school until the break, but there were days I was called to pick her up. When I got to the school, she was just sitting and rocking with tears in her eyes.

#207. LOST AT SCHOOL

They found her
In an empty classroom
On the floor
Doing a puzzle
In a haze
She's 13
I was called
She's in the counseling office
Not responding to words
Come on, come home
We'll try again tomorrow

#208. BUT FOR CHRISTY

Christy concluded that she was safer dead than alive.

"I'd rather be dead!"
She grabbed a bag
She decided to try
Over her head
Sucking in
To force the bag
Down her throat
Becca and I wrestle
Can't loosen her grip
But I rip the bag from the top
Yanking plastic
From her throat
She's determined
It's not about attention
Not a way to express
Her pain
Tangibly trying
Planning
What will be next

Elsie got the neighbors, and someone called for police. Honestly, I think I called. The officers came, approached slowly, and followed my lead. The 911 operator stayed on the line until they came in the door. I was holding Christy on the kitchen floor. My sister came and got the other girls; I was so glad she was old enough to drive and kind enough to drop everything for her nieces and me.

The police shared with the ER staff, I wasn't abusive. I skillfully talked the child down. They vouched for me. But my mind was busy. I felt like a telephone line that just keeps beeping: how am I going to address the other girls' issues and hope Ashley would be okay?

#209. WORDS TO CALM

Do you want to know what I told Christy as I sat on that floor? Words privy to the 911 responder?

"Christy, the police are coming. It's okay, Sweetie. It's okay. I know you are scared. I know you don't want them to see you like this. NO. You cannot grab that bag again. No. I'm going to hold your hands down. Christy, I need you to stop trying to bite me or I will need to change how I hold you. I don't want to hurt you accidently. STOP."

The officers called for an ambulance that took her to the hospital. She stayed in the hospital for a few days until she could be sent to a different one that had a children's psychiatric unit.

I could empathize; life, as she was experiencing it, felt worse than death. In her mind, she was being forced to decide if she could keep fighting or if she needed relief. The sad part was that, according to her limited reasoning, the only way to get relief was to die.

#210. SPLIT IN TWO

Within a few days, Christy was transferred to another hospital, one a few hundred miles away. She made the trip on Christmas Eve. The second hospital had a children's psychiatric unit (instead of just a bed in which to wait). I drove up the next morning. My parents had Ashley and Rebecca. A friend watched Elsie.

Before the clock could strike noon, my parents took Ashley to the hospital. She was so out of it that they didn't know if she had attempted to overdose. Dissociative kids can be hard to read. To put it in perspective, the first psychiatrist who treated Ashley said that he had never had a child more dissociative than her, in all his years of practice. The only children comparable were ones that had suffered extensive and ritualistic abuse. The events of the stalker, Christmas, a sister attempting suicide were more than she could face. She had gotten triggered and, for her, it felt safer to sleep outside on the snow than in bed.

In the hospital, they did a blood test and asked Ashley, "are you thinking about hurting yourself or others?" My daughter denied it. To which the hospital responded by telling my parents, her grandparents, that she was being discharged. However, my parents refused to take her home. They were adamant that she was still a danger to herself and others. As a result, I was called.

I had one hour to pick Ashley up or be charged with child abandonment. It would have taken me three to four hours to drive and get her, with no stops to pee. I was beyond irritated. These were the same people who a few hours back had told me to drive to the other hospital to admit Christy. They had told me that Christy needed a parent to be physically present when she was admitted at the other hospital.

So there I was. I had two kids in two hospitals in two different cities, a few hundred miles apart. There were some hard moments, but that day all I wrote, "Now. Now, I hurt. God, it is not humanly possible to be two places at once."

I sat on the floor of Christy's hospital room and asked myself (and the doctor) what I should do. The other hospital wanted to wait and admit Ashley after she seriously injured someone. If she ran into someone and they broke a leg or if she ran into the street and was killed. I'm being a bit facetious, but the idea was that she needed to seriously injure someone, not just have frostbite on her hands or bruises on her sister's leg.

If I did as they suggested, there was an impending risk. In a situation following a serious injury, it would go to child welfare, an organization that had previously thought the best plan was for Ashley to live with her dad.

I sat there with Christy and her doctor. What should I do? Ashley was only a danger when trauma triggered her. She wasn't just depressed or manic. As a parent, I wanted an approach that would protect both her, her sisters, and my family. I could not quietly wait until she ended up in foster care or, worse, with her dad.

I felt too raw to speak purposely, but I chanced it as I requested insight from Christy's psychiatrist. "Given the dilemma, what should I do? Should I lie? Or do I just wait until she hurts someone and ends up in Juvenile Detention or her dad's?"

I had never lied to a social worker or doctor before. Not talked, yes. Been crappy when frustrated by psych assessments, yes. But lied, no. I wondered if I even had the capacity to do it? Could I do it if it meant she would have the treatment she needed? If it was because it was in HER best interest?

I considered another solution. I could ask my parents to pick her up and wait with her in the waiting room instead of taking her home, then drive across the icy pass, and try to flood Ashley with triggers of her childhood, so that the ER would see her when she was in that state. They'd figure I was abusive and cruel, but they could see Ashley when she was triggered and might take the response into account if she went into foster care so she would not go to her dad's.

To purposely do that to a child, though, crap. Being cruel to my daughter, knowing she might rightfully hate me for that, in a final attempt to see her get the treatment for PTSD that she needs? That couldn't be my last option, right?

The psychiatrist wasn't fazed by my dilemma or my heartbroken solutions, or the irony of discussing lying to a doctor with him, a physician. Instead, he offered another option. All I had to do was get someone to pick up Ashley in an hour.

#211. CHRISTMAS SITTERS ARE HARD TO FIND

Finding someone available on Christmas day to host a dissociative kid seemed impossible. Almost everyone I knew had family and friends, or kids, over to celebrate. I laughed at the irony of celebrating Jesus' birth; just like Mary and Joseph, I was desperately seeking a place for my child.

If an Alzheimer's patient wandered out in the cold and fell asleep when it was below freezing or knocked people down stairs and didn't remember, there would be options, but not for a little girl with PTSD. I wanted to argue. It sucked, but I still needed someone so that I didn't risk her being sent by child welfare to live with Frank.

I still remember the prayer I said as I sat on the bench outside the hospital doors. I was so pissed at God for allowing such a mess. Eventually, it became a poem. God promises to be a husband to the widows, so I figured I would take Him at His word.

> God
> Please remember
> Ashley and Your
> promise
> To help me
> Parent

I can't get her and
If You serve as
My husband
I need You now
I don't need an image
Of You on a
Big comfortable cloud
As a cushion or couch
I need someone
Who can get her
And hold her
And love her
Because she needs it
Plus, I am about to be
Charged with
Abandonment
Do you want that
On my record?
You already had it once
Remember? Jesus?
Once is enough, right?
My family can't get her
Because they are afraid
She is too dissociative
To keep safe
I am over a hundred miles away,
With OUR other child, alone
So if You have
Any ornaments for the tree

I mean any

Ideas?

Of who is available

Christmas day

Willing to pick up a child

From the hospital

And babysit

Let me know

Call the church

The pastors can't do it

But there is a woman

A lonely woman with

Stage four cancer

A woman, who knows trauma

Alone and afraid

With no stairs in her house

Or a kid

She's more than willing

To share a companion

And she has alarms on her doors

And windows?

Good call

I don't have patience

For much more

Of this

That was a much better solution than forcing a kid with attachment issues and severe trauma to be ripped from her family after injuring herself or a sibling. That could have created another sociopath.

#212. FIGHTING

God, sometimes when we fight, I think I am just so filled with fear and anger and burden. I know I am hitting You with my words like fists. Thanks for just holding me so closely that I can't get hurt or hurt You in those moments. Thanks for calming my arms in the grip of a hug and not letting go until the pain breaks.

#213. RECONNECTING

God is not like Frank. He never forces adoration after a fight. He never demands I trust him; He simply remains present. He listens to my heart.

#214. CHRISTY'S NEEDS

But more importantly, the doctor had Christy in the hospital after attempting suicide and, without Ashley treated, he could not justify sending Christy back to the exact situation that triggered her suicidality. Ashley wasn't a danger to herself or others as long as she wasn't triggered. The problem was, there were A LOT of things that triggered her.

#215. LYING ALONE

After I had left the hospital that night, I got a call from Christy's psychiatrist. For whatever reason, I trusted him with the information of our lives. Looking back, I have wondered what caused me to be able to trust him with our story. It was one thing. He gained access to the seal of my trust when he could grapple with my utter honesty and mother's heart. If he could handle issues of immoral, but ethical decisions, he was safe.

I spent the night at a hostel with parents and families from all over the nation. Parents grieving for a child who was shot, another burned in a fire, children too sick to ever be able to live outside a hospital. I ate some dinner and went to my room to sleep.

Lying in bed, I gambled that maybe God could connect with me without causing pain. I ventured to test if He was safe.

God, I want to know You as
Saltwater knows the ocean
To fill You so profoundly
That Our boundaries flee

I want to sink to Your depths
And be swirled to Your side
I want to rise on the currents
And sway with the tide

God, can You create those patterns
Of movement in me?
Can You take the energy
You've created and make it move
With that type of fluidity?

Can You stir in me so softly
That You still leave the sediment to sink?
Can You move so gently that I
Can still fall asleep?

I'll let You try tonight,
If You promise
To creep.

I hurt a lot, but lying there, alone, I knew I had God with me.

#216. SOLUTION

The psychiatrist orchestrated a plan. He spoke with Ashley's pediatrician. She admitted Ashley to our home-town hospital. He called and said they had a bed for her in the other city's child psych unit. The ER worker rolled her eyes when Ashley came. She was visibly shocked when there was a bed available in a children's hospital with a psychiatric unit. Usually, those take at least a week to procure AND this was the kid who she kept discharging because Ashley never remembered her dissociative dramas.

It was nice working with a doctor who was intelligent, but more importantly wise. It was interesting to hear him speak, too. He used phrases from nine different cultures in one hour. Sometimes I tally those things. Regardless, he could speak the language of my kids and life.

I don't know how much longer I would have lasted without someone being able to listen and converse in those dialects. Every mother's heart needs people to listen to the whispers of her children especially when her children's cries have long since gone unanswered.

#217. ANOREXIC

During the week that followed Christmas, Becca stopped eating. That prompted my parents to send her up to stay with me. She'd at least eat a little when I was by her. I took her to the hospital with me. She saw Christy which thawed some of her reluctance. Christy's psychiatrist asked if he could speak with Rebecca privately. He could sense the sexual abuse.

She confided that she knows it happened, but she couldn't verbalize the details. He told her that she needed to start eating or he'd have to admit her, too.

And Elsie? During that time, I prayed that the upheaval would not shake her. That I would not have to unravel a deeper mess caused by the weekly instability.

#218. RECOVERING

With new medications on board, Ashley and Christy settle back into a routine. Attending school, playing in the snow with coats and gloves, and walking through the house without quite as much panic.

Elsie lost it a bit. She hurt. It had been hard to be uprooted and sent to a friend's house right before Christmas. She was young enough that she didn't know how to say that, so she mimicked Christy. Instead of suffocating herself with a bag, she locked herself in the bathroom and said she that she was going to commit suicide. She wanted my attention and time; she did not have any intention to commit suicide. It pissed me off to tell you the truth.

#219. ATTENTION

Stop
Stop now
I say
Don't you dare
Pick that up

Cleanse your mouth
And your heart
I am here
And I hear you
And I'll listen
My dear

But don't you dare
Pick that up
And wear it
For play

Not today
Not tomorrow
Let it lay

#220. FISHING

As things settled down, Christy discovered fishing.

My journal reads "She wakes me up at 5 am to go catch breakfast before school. The thrill of getting a fish hooked is addictive. It's nice to see her linking enjoyment, peace, and patience with reward. It's not that I love 5 am fishing, but I love seeing her so happy."

She caught so many that I needed to smoke some to eat later.

#221. SERVICES

The girls got into "Wraparound," basically they had a counselor that came to our home and skills trainers. The girls started physical therapy. Their muscle tone improved. They also did occupational therapy. It was nice to have other people carry some of the weight and see my kids improving in so many ways.

I got to spend a little time with friends and had some great discussions. One of my best friends was a linguist that had worked in the Army. She was fascinating and kind.

We got referred to Vision Therapy. There the doctor was able to test and show that the head injuries were causing Rebecca's headaches and nausea. She tested the other kids and me, with similar results. Hence, we started vision therapy.

#222. NAME CHANGE

With things going so well, I figured the girls were stable enough to change our last name. I had not done it when I got divorced because I felt the girls needed a sense of stability, and Frank would have never gone for divorce and name changes.

We looked up names, looked up meanings, and debated different ones. The girls started lots of email accounts, saving the name in case we decided it would be the one.

Changing my name was easy. It took about a month, but the girls had to have Frank's approval or have it go to court. Frank was flabbergasted. Why would they possibly not want his name? After too many hours, I asked, "I could have them just write you letters of why. Would that help?" I was shocked when he said "yes."

#223. EVEN THIS

I think I know why people say OM when they meditate. Over and over again. M-OM. The reality of life. Birth, nurturing, and death.

I keep telling myself, "I will make it through even this." Deep breath in, pause and repeat.

I sat them down and gave each one a piece of paper.

#224. CLUES OF ABUSE

Over the years, various clues made me wonder if he had abused the girls. He looked at pornography while holding Christy on his lap. He lost his job more than once for looking at pornography. I would always know before he was discretely fired, because Becca would start compulsively masturbating on the dining room chairs until she bled.

Sometimes he would come home when Ashley was changing her clothes; she would run outside and hide in the dog house as fast as she could. Oddly, he was adamant that no one hurt his girls, yet he harmed them repeatedly. But the biggest clue, he had said he was spanking our unborn baby as he beat me when I was pregnant.

#225. LETTERS

The girls' letters were blunt. Never ask articulate young ladies to explain why they don't want to share the name of their abuser if you don't want honesty. It was evident I was not the one forcing them to change their last name.

I snapped a picture of each one and emailed the replicas to Frank. The originals I sent to Child Welfare, before giving copies to the girls' counselor. Of course, she had to report it to Child Welfare as well. Good. Abuse should be reported.

#226. INQUIRY

Child welfare came by, as did a State Police officer, to talk to the girls. They were not currently being abused, so Child Welfare closed that part of the investigation.

The supervised visitation center staff worked with the other offices and provided their own observations. So, instead of going to court for any other reason, we went to change our name. My father came to the hearing dressed up like a biker, leather jacket and all, ready to protect if Frank came to object.

One funny thing happened when I went to turn in the forms requesting the hearings. I went in through the metal detector to get the forms, then I left. A few hours later, I returned. I had changed my boots because the ones I wore that morning let rain seep in. The second time, I set off the detectors. The sheriffs had seen me earlier go through, so they were on guard. Did I have a knife? A gun? No, Italian homemade leather boots, apparently with metal inside.

#227. DISCONNECT

The State Police officer went to speak to Frank. Frank claimed he could not understand why the girls would want to change their names. The officer asked, "Have you seen the letters?" He had seen them, read them, yet could not fathom why our girls would not want his last name. The officer just looked at me and shook his head. All he could do was exclaim, "WTF, I just don't get it."

"Only from the mouth of a sociopath," I rationalized. No one else would be able to be blamed for sexual and physical abuse and still not see why those abused would not want to share a last name.

Frank had also called the girls' counselor. She had written a letter supporting the girls' decisions and stating that each girl had individually chosen the change. He refused to meet when she said she could only talk to him about it in person.

#228. ABUSE INVESTIGATION

When the State Police officer first came to our home. He was planning on talking mainly with Becca, but within a few minutes realized, the issue was not just with one kid. Becca was just the most detailed in her letter.

An appointment was scheduled for Becca to be interviewed by a team skilled in working with kids and the topic of abuse. But the night before her interview, she broke down. She had never cut herself before, but that night, she cut herself over twenty-five times. Each cut over five inches, crisscrossing her inner thighs from her knee to her vagina.

I took her into the scheduled appointment. Within just a few minutes it became apparent she was too unstable and suicidal to be interviewed. A police car took her to the hospital.

#229. JAPANESE CRANES

I started folding origami cranes with the prayer that suicide's allure would finally break. Becca stayed a week. She was discharged before there was an opening in another hospital with psychiatric unit for kids.

I thought back to the supervised visitation center's Christmas party. One of the workers had convinced me to attend. He dared say, "Sometimes the best thing you can offer is a working life." He was referring to mine. Even thinking about it, I just shake my head. However, it was his and the other staff's encouragement that gave me the strength to not stop trying.

#230. BODIES SPEAK

My acupuncturist told me
When he is sad
He talks to his father
I think he meant
His Father in prayer
I spoke to his father
A few years back
And was amazed by what

I didn't have to say
His father could read
My pulse in a way
That taught him far more
Than words, even perfect
Could ever portray

He was also the only man to stand up to Frank during the abuse. For the most part, I had only heard him speak Chinese; his son translated for him. But Frank drove me to an appointment one day, with four children in tow.

The acupuncturist took my pulse and looked at Frank. The intensity of his eyes could have pierced metal armor. "She has 'nother baby. She die. You kill her."

Whoa. That was a man I could trust.

#231. APPROACH

Our culture tries to get women to leave
Their marriages
To overthrow authority
Malicious authority, sure
But some women believe
To trust and submit

Instead of just aiming at women
Empowerment
Men need to stand up and say
Real men don't harbor
That shit

Violence, abuse
We'll take you out
If you act like that

Maybe that is too violent, but if abuse were a dialect, it might be appropriate. You have to speak in ways that people understand.

#232. VISITORS

Becca was allowed family visitors at the hospital. She wanted her God Mother, Lillie. I pondered how I could manage that. Lillie's response, write her name and for the relation: fairy-godmother, no one would argue with that. She was right; they didn't.

#233. INTERPLAY

If I were a rock
Crystal I'd be
And bend light to Your eyes
In response

Oh, God
Rape made me
Bound
If only I could
Play with You still

But today
All I can do is
Lay my body here
Next to You
And wish to reflect
Your rays

Your dream I hold up
In the hope that
Your power
Could give wings
To my matter
To dance

And like my kind fairy
Please land very lightly
(just in case)
We touch

God, I don't even have the energy to think about interacting yet. But if You can lead me, please just go slow.

#234. GROWING

God, I want to share my life with You, my experiences, and the things I have learned. I want You to taste what I have made of them, the things You have thrown at me, the pain. I've learned to bend it, to make it new. I learned how not to hurt, how to use it all.

I always wondered why You would give those things to me, but they are ideal for building. You couldn't give them to me Yourself. You couldn't bear to hurt me. Did You know their power? The power of pain, disillusionment, and shame? Did You know they could be overcome?

#235. REVOLUTION

Rebecca ended back in the hospital. She had gone to see her pediatrician who then sent her straight to the ER. The other girls could stay home. I had the chance to take a shower, wear pajamas to bed, and cry.

#236. THE SKY

For whatever reason, even with the cataplexy treated, I still could get so weak that it affected my breathing. Sometimes, people talk about God healing as if they pray and demand what they want. The forcefulness of their faith being so important that they forget God. But healing can be slow, gradual. And ultimately, we all die.

I wrote my prayer as a poem:

> Your sky is so intimate
> It kisses, embraces
> It knows every move
> Every breath
> As it holds
> Me
> It fills the space
> Around me

Perfectly tracing my skin

And it whispers

To my lips

God

I'm scared

I'm going to stop

Breathing again, when the blows

Are too much

Can we share?

Be there on the air

Right outside of my lips

To force a full breath

Back inside

Regardless of the cause, emotional or physical, God was the only doctor who could treat the part from abuse.

#237. INNOCENCE

Is there an innocence that was there before them that I don't remember? Is that what is so special? I can't grasp it anymore, I hope that is okay. Or have You provided something new? Is it wisdom and grace that covers me now, like a shawl protecting one from the wind?

Does it matter to You? Do You miss my childhood? Or do You still love me the same? As I do You? Oh, I have missed You, my God. I feel like the experiences have made Our love richer. In the past, I could sense You, see You, feel You in the just and I could sense You and see You and feel Your warmth when life was unjust, but I couldn't see You in the depths of pain—not pulling me out, but in pain itself. It's like I felt Your pain. I don't mean to be rude, but God, Your pain is a mess.

There is an innocence in my children that's lost. I see it and I wish they could have it back.

#238. THE ER SOCIAL WORKER

I think she just doesn't like me. But I, like the truth, can just be myself. If there are things I can change that might help, would You refine them in me? Or would You help her? Even with the pediatrician, counselor, and supervised visitation center staff all reassuring her that it's not just me taking the kids for a night off, she struggles.

I don't think it is as hard for me as her. I just want to help my kids make it through this alive. I don't need her to like me, but it is hard to see her coloring change when she should admit the girls. I feel badly that she struggles. All I ask, God, just don't it affect the outcomes for my children. That is the line I draw.

#239. STUPID

The girls' new physical therapist decided she would cross the line of her scope of practice by suggesting to Becca that she should write a letter forgiving her dad. The physical therapist went on to share her own experience with an abusive father. There is a reason scope of practice exists. Becca refused to go back.

#240. GRADUAL CHANGE

The girls can tolerate talking for 2-5 minutes about any "real issues" with their counselor before they dissociate or leave. I have always held a two-minute rule with them. They can only talk about the past for that long before I say they have to speak to a therapist. I could not have them triggering each other, or me. Plus, I just wanted a house that had interesting conversations about the present and future. Safe conversations. So maybe their inability to talk was caused by me.

Thinking about it, I probably would have been criticized if I allowed past issues to dominate my home. Good thing I didn't have the need to keep everyone happy. Being autistic can help at times.

#241. ME

I am like a jewel that has a lot of different sides. I am simple-minded, yet intelligent. I am kind, yet clueless. I am spiritual, but at times blasphemous. I am curious, yet easily bored. I don't fit into a prelabeled box. I think it confuses people. There is a certain freedom that comes with autism. There is no pressure to conform to society's labels. You can just be yourself.

#242. CONTENT

There is a contentedness and sense of peace that come with knowing You even when everything is astray.

#243. A THOUSAND IDEAS

My optometrist suggested
Talking to a neurologist
My eyelids kept drooping
I went and was tested
Not everything is about my girls
I'm amazed
How many ways
Can a body be weak?
Is there a way for every day
Of the week?
Sheesh.

The neurologist put me on Mestinon, a medication for myasthenia along with giving me the diagnosis. But instead of getting stronger, I got much weaker. I needed oxygen and a hospital bed. Despite the vulnerability, I have never felt calmer; not a muscle held tension. Lying in the hospital bed, I had to rest just to have strength to draw in each single breath.

[To be kind to all the doctors who are reading this book, here is a spoiler alert]... Later, another neurologist would solve the puzzle: slow channel congenital myasthenia with treatments that also treat cataplexy.

I think my case would be the best doctorate-degree, extra credit problem for differential diagnosis EVER: a patient with autism, history of trauma, muscle weakness, narcolepsy from a sleep study, and low oxygen. She can't figure out jokes or tell them, so try to trigger the cataplexy correctly. She is not always able to follow those simple commands about movement and gets confused by gradient scales. She has a severe history of abuse and does not like being touched... I could go on.

Be honest now. How many doctors would have just rolled their eyes and written it off as conversion disorder or some weird autism avoidance thing? I am glad that my doctors did not.

Life is much easier with enough oxygen to run my brain, the ability to stay awake for an entire grocery store trip, and the strength to screw in a light bulb. I still don't get jokes, but I can laugh at my own, which my kids think is funny. The new cataplexy test: she can speak autistic babble, find it funny, and laugh without her jaw going slack, but still doesn't respond to the things that make everyone else laugh.

#244. NEXT

Christy was in the hospital next. Honestly, I stopped trying to remember the reasons she was admitted. I am sure it had something to do with depression, anxiety, or medication. However, she was also hospitalized with breathing problems at points, too.

I wanted to cry, hold up in a hole, and disappear. I felt like a Band-aid that had gotten ripped off so many times that I lost my stickiness. I knew I should care, but I was numb.

The only thing I remember was the police officer asking, after he transported her to the hospital,

> "Is this one a runner?"
> I looked at him in disbelief
> She had no shoes on
> He wore shoes with arches

Her legs were shorter
He looked like he even exercised

But I smiled
"She might, but I think you could catch her."

In my mind
I laughed
I have caught these kids
Barefoot, on rocks
With shards of glass
I'd caught Ashley
Weeks after giving birth
As I peed my pants
He could manage just fine

#245. WORDS

God, he beat my children
He raped them, they say
As they open up
God, did You hear that?
Why did You allow that?
What was there to prove?
Couldn't he have just stopped with me?
I'm still mad about that.

I debate with the girls' counselor. Maybe they just don't know what the word rape means? I need to believe. Not them, but my denial.

#246. GOD'S PAIN

Sometimes I wonder the pain that You felt when we were going through that. What shame You felt to have created a universe where that happens. People all over the world throughout history that cried out to You the same, You heard everyone. Constantly, hearing that scream for decades, centuries, millennia, with no reprieve. I am certain that at least one person has been in the state of being raped, or beaten, somewhere on Earth every moment for centuries.

Talk about regret. I know that cry, I felt it. To have to listen to it CONSTANTLY, how do You not cover Your head and sink? Those people, men and women, who shared that cry, I know You were there for them as You were for me. I know You heard, even if You can't say it. I promise, God, it will be okay. I'll carry You in that pain.

#247. UP A TREE WITHOUT A LADDER

Christy was released from the hospital. By four in the afternoon, she was on the roof wanting to jump off. You have to love medicine changes. That's sarcasm, again, if it isn't clear. I talked her down, distracting her with Legos. But as the short-acting medication wore off, she got more and more impulsive. She still wanted to die.

Life was just more than she could deal with emotionally. She ran off. With her sisters' help, we managed to herd her back toward the house. Next, she went vertical, again, up an old decaying tree to the top. She wasn't rational. She was traumatized wanting any way to escape life.

As dusk approached and the temperature dropped, she just freaked. I don't remember calling 911, but the police, ambulance, fire truck, and rescue truck came.

The police came first. It was evident that they had gone through extra mental health trainings.

They positioned themselves around the tree, responding in ways to be non-threatening. They asked, "What has worked in the past? What are her interests?" Legos.

It was heartwarming to hear all that those officers had to say about Legos. In police training, maybe there should be improv night. Draw a topic from a bowl of something a kid might like, then carry on a conversation while using body language (subdued body language) to lower the threat level of someone in a uniform with a gun. Whoever trained those guys, they knew what they were doing.

The rescue team came next. Men familiar with exertion, able to climb trees. But each time one would try to go up, even a bit, she would freak and climb higher. They formed a circle, in case the branch she was on snapped. They could try to buffer her fall. She looked like a cornered animal, frantically trying to escape.

They tried a ladder from the firetruck, but she pushed it away from the tree, panicking they would reach her, touch her, hurt her. The men had a good hold on the ladder, but they were concerned that she might fall as she let go of a branch with one of her hands.

They tried distracting her by talking as one of the crew climbed the back side of the tree. As night fell, darkness sat down. They brought out a light as if forcing the night to stand until their task was complete. God vs. 30 men. Men won.

They just had to capture the fear in Christy's heart. It wasn't a case in which a kid had climbed too high. This one was traumatized and was not scared of falling, being injured, or dying. The head crew leader finally solved the riddle.

"I am going to climb half way up. For each step you take down, I will take a step down, too, and I will make one of these guys go away." With that, he had a deal. He orchestrated a plan that captured her fear of men, excitement, and being trapped. Sometimes, removal of presence can be a bargaining chip.

#248. JUST GIVE ME LESS

Sometimes, when I, or a child, is overwhelmed, it feels as if every sense is so heightened it screams. People can need everything to be LESS. Removal of presence, demands, and noise. It's why I like swimming, floating with my ears underwater, my eyes resting shut, and every inch of my skin feeling just one sensation: water.

#249. RESIDENTIAL TREATMENT

The hospital sent Christy to a residential treatment center and stayed there for two weeks. Room checks were every 15 minutes to ensure she did not hurt herself. It was a safe place where the doctors could increase the dosage of a new medication until it worked.

The psychiatrist there asked me to fill in the gaps about the abuse; I told him I couldn't. I suggested he speak with the girls' counselor back home and signed releases for the supervised visitation center as well.

My heart cried for
Not being able to talk yet

All I could say:

"I can tell you what I can

In passing as things come up

But if you want a detailed account

I would need to be in a place

Where I could grieve

Throw things

Mentally lose it, and fall apart

I have not been afforded that luxury

Quite yet, I must keep it together

Because I am the one who is holding

These four girls' lives

In my hands

I can't do that and rip

Our story out from the depths of

My heart

Where I buried it

In keeping us alive

He honored the honesty. The social worker and he both commented that I was insightful and helpful even though I could not delve down and drudge up Christy's youth.

Inside, I still say, "I can't tell them what I didn't see. I can't blame someone for what I hope I dreamed." But I also remember Frank's words, "I really did it," when I tried to deny what he did to me.

My children, I just can't go there, yet. I can't face it because that would mean I failed them when I was trying so hard to keep them safe. I felt like an ambulance driver who lost his first patient. I couldn't prevent it. I couldn't change it, but I wish I could. So I looked at them and tried to focus on what I could do right then. It's all any of us can do.

#250. MY CHILDREN

My children's bodies
Know many languages
Temperature
Volume
Are they hot or cold
Loud or bold
They speak color
Their skin shouting out
Is their circulation smooth

They speak attention and interest
As they reach out
Or startle
They speak overwhelmed
As they look away
Or grimace

They speak moisture
They speak movement and speed
Reaction to change
But they still need to
Speak rhythm

Consistency in their

Nervous systems
Peace and calmness
To digest foods
Mellowing to rest
And sleep

Those are languages
They still need
To speak

#251. MY BODY SPEAKS, TOO

I remember the day the girls wrote the letters to their dad about changing last names. I wrote about it, matter-of-factly, because I can't share my feelings about it and be logical at the same time.

That afternoon, after I sent the copies and talked with the girls' counselor, I went to my parents' house. I told them and cried. My dad, the sweetheart, asked what he could do. Just sit with me, hold me, let me cry.

I remember laying my head on his chest and weeping. I listened to his heartbeat and tried to settle mine to his rhythm. I tried to calm my breathing to the rise and fall of his chest as if they were tides in the ocean coming and going. I tried to let his body do for mine what I try to do for my girls when they need soothing.

A half hour later, I was still crying, but my sister (the one my girls called Baby Aunt, not the one that could already drive) had to be picked up from school. My dad motioned to my mother to take his place while he drove to the school. At this point, it gets a little funny.

People often assume I would have trouble feeling safe around men, because of Frank. What they don't know is my dad is a great guy. When I was little, I would swing with him in a hammock and talk; to top it off, swinging made my autistic body happy. He was awesome. If I scraped my knee, he would get a Band-Aid, no talking needed.

My mother is awesome, too, but our relationship is different. Let me put it this way, when I went to her with a scraped knee, she would tell me "That is your patella" ensuring I would be intelligent with a well-endowed vocabulary. But what she didn't realize was, I was autistic. If you don't know much about autism, autistic people are VERY literal. I thought it was funny that she would say that the answer to a scraped knee was my dad. "Pa tells all," was what I heard. I thought it was the coolest joke ever, because my dad didn't even talk when he fixed a knee! Regardless, as a child, I had two wonderful parents and nothing had changed that.

There I was, now sitting with my mom, a powerhouse of a woman with great leadership, teaching, and lecturing skills, but not a natural nurturer. She tried, don't get me wrong. I'm certain that if she could have paid a billion dollars to know how to be still and hold me, despite her own heart squeezing in her chest, she would have gone back in time, established a business to make billions, and saved the money for that moment.

Just sitting, with me, in pain. It was too unbearable, so she started offering suggestions. "Maybe if you look at it this way…" "What if you tell yourself it will be okay? We'll get through this." But what I needed was silence. I needed to be held. I didn't need a solution. I didn't need new ways to think. So I told her, "I don't need different ways to process this experience; I just need to feel this pain." She held me as I cried, and we both sat in discomfort. As I said, she was willing to do anything just to be there at that moment with me.

#252. HELPING THE GRIEVING

I know I do not respond to things like "normal" people. I don't understand sympathy or read the body language of concern, but I have something I would like to share about sitting with the grieving. I think it is true whether someone just got awful news or their loved one died.

You sit with me
I cry or maybe
I hold it inside
Fighting not wanting you to hurt
As I feel instinctively
Your body responding
Averting your eyes
Sharing the unease
Of grief
A tug-of-war of emotions
Pain and sadness
Pleading their case
But inside
Battling
Not wanting you to hurt, too
Knowing your body feels it
How should a friend
Respond?

It is at that moment that people screw it up. With one word, "advice." Really, just don't. Instead:

Allow yourself to feel
The discomfort
The unease
The fear of breaking
Because it hurts
So much
To see someone you love
Grieve

I'm autistic. I shouldn't know that, right? But empathy, feeling the same thing as others and knowing what they would like, is a joke. Want to be empathetic, ask "What would comfort YOU?" Pay attention to what is happening with their body without having the same chemicals in your own. Respond to the person. Reflexively feeling and assuming they want what you'd want, that is the easy way. God bless you if you can do it. But if not, you can still learn.

What do you do
When you feel someone's grief
What can you do to
Make it stop?
You can't

That feeling
That desperation
Forcing you
Compelling you
To advise

You are just feeling
The other person's grief
It's empathy
That makes you speak
You want to change it

But the lesson
In grief
The pain is that they can't
You can't
No one can change it
They can't go back
And cause someone
Not to die
Or stop something that happened

There is nothing
That anyone
Can do
To mitigate the pain

I do a thing I call "eating emotion." I am sure that the name will cause confusion. It has nothing to do with eating because of feelings. It's something I visualize when I am with someone who has emotions too large for one body.

I imagine my body connected with theirs. Maybe holding their hand, giving a hug, or simply sharing the air as we breathe. If you have ever breathed out on a cold winter day, you know that our breath goes a lot farther than we can smell. I imagine their emotions as chemicals forcing them to feel their physical intensity. And instead of speaking, I silently offer to drain off part of the current and let my body process that pain for them instead, let my body consume and process some of what they are feeling. Maybe it is what you all do, anyway, you just forget and speak. Speaking, by the way, is like burping those chemicals right back in the person's face.

Processing the chemicals for them, subduing them with your own, lets you touch just a bit of their pain. Regulating your response. Breathing deeply. Relaxing the tension. Centering yourself. Those things naturally help the other person control their body. It is truly the answer to "Be with me, in pain." Just share a little bit, so they aren't quite so alone.

The truth, that concept is the ultimate wisdom of compassion and the true heart of empathy. Settling someone's heart with your own. Calming a child's heart by regulating your own, that is a skill worth having. Patiently waiting as their body speaks pain and unease to yours and your body speaks "Even this can be managed with time and friends."

There are emotions, experiences, which are simply too much for one body to feel by itself. Those are the ones that need to be carried in love by others. It's an honor that truly needs no words.

#253. EXPECTATIONS

Healing from trauma is like grieving the death of a friend. Your losses, hopes, and shattered expectations consume you for a time.

#254. MOVING

Over the summer, we moved.

I mean for that period to be there. We moved. Period.

My girls and I relocated to a larger city, one with more services for traumatized and depressed youth. We could not handle the instability of being bounced between cities for treatment. I was desperate; I never wanted to see another hospital emergency room EVER in my entire life!

That spring, I had taken a textural painting class. It felt calming to do something, anything, that there was no way to mess up. I could just add another layer. I sincerely hoped life could be that way, too. Layers of healing transforming the layer of pain.

I've heard people talk about onions, comparing them to layers to work through in counseling. I like textured paintings better. The imagery gives clients greater control of what happens, and it allows survivors to dream instead of fear perpetually more of the same stinging truth.

#255. THE NIGHT THAT SEALED IT

I held Becca
Cradled in my arms
As she squirmed and fought
With a nightmare
Trying to make sense
Of life

Despite everything
That I had gone through

After the Violence

I had never had to
Figure out terror
With a child's heart

All I could do
Be the calm that she
So desperately craved
I held my "baby"
At the base of my bed
Praying that she could
Settle the flashbacks
With enough peace
To choose and face
The sunrise
Again

Elsie heard sister's cries
And begged to be held
But I couldn't
Hold both

Get down the heating blankets
From Mema and Poppa
Plug them in and let
Those blankets hold you
Instead

So in a pile
Ten feet from me

Elsie slept
Cradled by her grandparents
Love
While I cried

We got through that night
And a few more
Before I took Becca
Back to her doctor

The pediatrician sent her
Right back
To the hospital
Which then in turn
Sent her to be treated
At the hospital
A few hundred miles
Away

#256. SUICIDE AND THE CREST OF COURAGE

She lays there
Motionless
Eyes glazed over
Waiting to die

God, there is a difference between
Kids who say "suicide" because
They crave attention

Or shock
Or revenge, and those

Those who are suicidal.
Who don't care if you
Catch them, because
They'll just try again

Determination
A great thing
But, God, how can I grab it?
How can I reach
Way down in her soul
And grab hold of that fire?
The one I can't see

God, I look in her eyes and
I know it is there
But it's gone

Rekindle that flame
That desire to live
Rekindle that flame
Or
Let it be me
Let it be me that carries that shame
Let it be me whose spirit goes out
Let it be me
Kill my self

I've carried that burden
And captured that pain
I've faced death
And recovered
I've taken that blame

So, my God, I beg
Steal my spirit
In quiet this night
And enter her body
And let it fight

Fight for her freedom
Her hopes and her dreams
Fight for her honor
Go now, with
Me

#257. ANY WAY POSSIBLE

Becca made the journey in by secure transport, so she could not run or try to hurt herself during the trip. I drove the family van. I didn't realize when I left that it would be the last time I would see that town for over a year.

Becca stayed in the hospital for over two weeks. The doctor, who had spoken to her when her sister Christy was hospitalized, was still there. He took her case.

I had left our home filled with every belonging, dishes undone, laundry piled up; as anyone with a loved one in the hospital knows, dishes or laundry are just not the priority. There are many ways that my family has helped through time, but that summer they won an award.

First, they watched Becca's sisters. When that started to draw out, they drove the girls to stay with me. As it became clear that we could not handle the stress, being bounced around among cities, they packed up our whole home. Our entire home, every plate, every freshly washed garment, every bed. Then, they sold that house and bought another one for the girls and me to rent in the city with psychiatric units for kids, day treatment schools, counseling and skills training, and all the other things we might ever need.

When Becca was released from the hospital, I spoke with the insurance. They were willing to cover all four girls going to a day treatment school. It felt like having had a broken arm for weeks and finally getting a cast. We only had to wait a month for openings. I'd like to say everything went smoothly for four meager weeks, but I can't.

#258. CHRISTY AND A ROAD

Christy is still intent that she should be dead
It's exhausting
She ran into a street today trying to get hit by a car
I called the crisis line as I corralled her to a little
Community garden
Four lanes of traffic
Did they need to call the police?
No, just be on the phone if it teeters that way
Fortunately, there was a bug in that garden

God, are You here
Even here?

In the crap of trying to keep
Multiple suicidal kids safe?
Be the bug
Make it interesting
God, You can do that, right? Be a bug
Just capture my child's traumatized kid's heart
So she doesn't get hit by a car

I am so tired of trying to figure this out
Can You carry that one for a while
So I can get the other two
And the hospital can get Becca?

#259. INTERSTATE

I was driving down the interstate at 65 mph when a song came on the ra-
dio that Frank used to love. Christy pulled at the door and tried to get out.
I don't know if people understand that post-traumatic stress disorder isn't
rational. It humbles even intelligent adults to the most basal reactions. As
her sisters pulled her back, I took the next exit. We had the child safety
latches activated, but a kid trying to get out of a car, that is just not safe. In
my mind, I knew she should be hospitalized or in the residential program.
I could not even get her across town safely. I've since learned audiobooks
in the car prevent flashbacks from songs. But at the time, I didn't dare tell
the doctors. I just could not deal with another hospitalization. I knew it
was selfish, but I just couldn't.

#260. REALISTICALLY

Being positive or optimistic just don't feel honest right now. I wonder if people misunderstand optimism. Could it be that optimism is about seeing options, even if you don't like any of them? There is a freedom in being grateful for choices even when they all seem unpleasant or challenging. In even the worst of situations, there exists the option to walk through it grudgingly, and there exists an opportunity to walk through it with grace. Optimism for me is not about believing the future is great, but believing that I at least get to choose my attitude with it.

#261. BUGS

I found a journal in the garage today, resting on top of one of the hundred boxes I need to unpack. The move was worth it. Christy wrote, "I love our new home. There are so many bugs and spiders." Pages upon pages of diagrams depicting every web in the yard with detailed observations regarding web strand width, the types of bugs each spider prefers, even how each responded when she added snails and bugs into their webs. She's content. It makes the move worth it.

#262. RUNAWAY

But even with the peace she got from bugs, she still tried to run off with knives and a backpack. I don't think she thought it through, but hey that fits with the spirit of impulsivity and trauma. It was the night before she would start at her new school. Anxiety convinced her it would be better to run off and kill herself than face a new school.

As the sun went down, I found her. I called the crisis number that I was provided for situations like these. The person on duty decided to call the police and an ambulance. I also asked them to call the counseling center that was supposed to start serving the girls.

The police came first. By the time they got there, I had separated Christy from the backpack that housed the knife and pinned her to the ground. The officers were not trained to deal with kids in a crisis. They tried shaming her, telling her she was acting like a two-year-old. That runaways were not really important. If she ran away again, they would just take a report on a piece of paper. But the worst, they had more important things to do than help a child who wanted to die.

The EMTs came next. Their approach was much different. Instead of belittling her or telling me it was not a police matter, they asked what would be best for my child. My hope at the time was that she would be able to stay and attend her new school in the morning.

Part of me wished I could crawl under a rock. This pattern: police, EMTs, hospitals HAD TO STOP. Fortunately, the next man to arrive was able to break that incessant revolving door. All of society should thank him for the money he saved treating my girls respectfully and competently. They still had to go to day treatment school, don't get me wrong, but he managed to counsel Christy and have all three sisters on his caseload.

He arrived and promised the EMTs to stay until she was stable or call them again. When the ambulance left and the knives were locked up—can I just interject that moving an entire house and unpacking everything can make keeping dangerous things away just a bit of a challenge—we made a spot for a blanket campout in our new house's garden. Grass covered with blankets, locked out of the house, we spent that night in the yard.

As we laid there, she sobbed out that the thought of school was just too much; she couldn't deal with the lights and people talking inside. We found a safe spot with her spiders and bugs. It's not what would make me feel safe, but to her, they were family.

#263. THANK YOU

Dear wise ambulance driver
Thank you
For giving her time
To calm down

Thank you
For listening
And respecting
Our life

Thank you
For helping her
Figure out how
She could make
It to school
Make it through
One more night

We slept
Under a tree
In a yard
Full of spiders

The on-call counselor who had come to help did a fact off about bugs. His knowledge of bugs relaxed her insecurity and she began to feel safe. He went in the house and worked with her sisters so they could go to bed, too.

#264. TO THE OFFICERS

I understand that you were trying your best. You were a bit frustrated with the situation and needed some training. I appreciate that you came, but there is something you might want to consider.

Shame does not motivate a kid who is scared. I was glad that the crisis line called you; I needed you to be present and move the backpack farther away. But you should know this, these calls and your approach do matter.

#265. UNTRAINED WORDS

> Your words
> Might work with
> Your kids
> The ones you've cared for
> Since birth
> Who look up to you
> And want
> To please you
> But those words
> Do not work
> For
> Never will work
> For

Kids that are hurting
And used to shame
They've already
Been
Mocked
And made to feel
Lame

I heard the truth of what those officers said. Christy had regressed under pressure. But the truth was, she didn't need truth right then, she needed safety.

There was another thing they needed to know. The effort they put into each interaction, no matter how seemingly inconsequential, has the power to save officers HUNDREDS of hours of work in the future. The way a kid views them will influence that child's interaction with police for years to come.

Are police safe? Do they serve kindly? Do I matter?

Each seemingly inconvenient call holds a value. At the next "important" call that you get, ask yourself, "At what point could we have intervened before it got to this point?" I'd much rather have you inconvenienced babysitting a freaking out adolescent until a crisis worker gets there than cutting her body down from a rafter. The calls that waste your time contain an opportunity to reach through time and change someone's fate.

I realize that it's easy to get worn and jaded, but please, try to dust off that rubble. You are needed, and I appreciate your service.

#266. HUMAN TELEGRAM FOR A DAY

Can I be a personal telegram from You? I want people to hear my story and feel You instead of the depression and pain that typically is felt in the wake of abuse.

I already write thank you cards to people each year on either Christmas or my birthday. I sit down and ponder which five individuals have impacted my life the most that year. I've written to neighbors, food banks, police officers, doctors, counselors, family members, and philanthropists. I'm wondering if my presence, instead of just letters on a page, could say thank you to those around me.

My life doesn't feel like a thank you card. It is demanding and frustrating. I am not sure how to share my thankfulness with those who have been part of it. I don't know how to embrace all the challenges and still let people know how thankful I am for them being part of my journey. Are there other individuals who know how to do that? People who would have known how if they lived my life?

#267. MY SHOES

Try lack of sleep from nightmares
Lack of digestion from constant stress
Try head injuries
Pain, bruises, dislocated joints
Try confusion from misappropriated authority
Being blamed by society for doing
Everything wrong
Try being judged for your decisions, when

After the Violence

You try, but your memory and judgment are impaired
From abuse

Vets who act like that are considered
Depressed, traumatized, scared, but
Worthy of our respect
For their service, dedication, and time
I am trying to serve, to overcome, to think
Doing my best
But women coming out of abuse
We are judged a bit harshly

Needy
Lazy
Stupid
Craving attention
Manipulating

And on top of the judgments
Add caring for children
Constantly trying
Attempting
To keep
Basic safety
Survival
Figuring out
Shelter and food
Companionship
Things abusers provide

Try not making sense
Feeling confused
And then having people mad
When you are not
Rational
When your life
Doesn't make sense
But you just keep on
Trying

Tell me that is not
A hard job
Afforded respect
Then on top of that
There is pain
In seeing
Your constant demand

Wishing people
Could see beauty
And thankfulness
From the walk
Of your day

#268. THANK YOU

My request is this, until people see a life that makes sense, please tell them
how grateful we are. Tell them that their service is valued. I want them to

know that, even when my service is not seen or appreciated. Please help me write thank you cards with ink until they can read the impact of their dedication in my family's life.

#269. QUIET AS SLIPPERS

There is another thing about my shoes; they whisper to God. Even when I try to step silently, He knows. Sometimes I try to hear His footsteps as well. I know He must be busy with all that HE has to do, but I still try to listen. It was so freeing to have the girls held securely by the treatment team. I finally got to enjoy playing with God and healing instead of just asking, demanding, begging for solutions.

> I feel like a girl playing seek with a crush
> My ears so in tune with each step
> My eyes are shut, I promise: I peek
> Oh God, You know me too well
> But I jest. I want to count out loud
> I do. But I don't want to muffle
> Any sound that could lead me
> To You, so, if I find a way to slip
> Them inside, please just be silent and
> Let me sit with my pride

I might not have embraced spiders like Christy did, but I loved swaying in the hammock in front of our house.

#270. HENNA

Instead of cutting herself, Becca has been drawing intricate patterns on her skin with Henna or a washable marker.

#271. TEASING GOD

You are the drops of water that fall
From the tree
Long after
It has stopped
Raining

Tickling me with Your pause
Even if it takes a minute
I trust calmness will come
Do You like
Playing with time?

#272. A THANK YOU LETTER

I wrote a thank you card a few years back to someone. He said it was the first thank you card he had ever received in his line of work. I found it sad, to be honest. I am sure he has received more. He most likely didn't know how to read them. A smile of a child, the relief of a parent, the police officers who were spared years of a depressed and violent teen. Please help people see the impact of their work and aid those who receive to calm their current life drama and be grateful for the service.

#273. NEEDS

When we relocated, we had several needs: confidentiality, experienced counselors, and time to heal. It took a while to secure all of those, but it happened. Eventually, I could just relax.

#274. JUST A THOUGHT

It is easy to cast blame on a parent
But it takes skill to collaborate instead
Regardless, if blamed just stay
Centered
People are perplexed by the
Emotional maturity of not responding
I learned that early on

A word of advice, when working with families like mine, if you choose to play the judge, you will never succeed. That is a role, with a very high fee, that only God can do and succeed.

#275. GOD THINKS OF EVERYTHING

God, how is it that, as I remember and the pain gets too much, You seem to fill me with the power of a poppy, a delirium of visions of You? You always catch me when my past attempts to make me fall. How do You do that? You have a drug that dealers can't make, don't You? O, my sweet Man, You truly think of everything.

#276. EVENING WALK

Becca and I went to the park this evening. We do it a lot, just stroll and talk. It was raining so hard the drug dealers weren't even there. At least, that is what I first thought. You don't have to buy to know them; their actions scream their intent. I was wrong. They just were sitting in their cars. Ludicrous, if you ask me. God, please give my girls courage and reinforce their ability to face life on its terms, so they do not go down that path.

#277. PHONE WARS

I was on the phone with the crisis line today. Becca had lost it. During the call, the crisis worker commented, "I think we have a bad connection." There was nothing wrong with the line. She just didn't know Becca.

My daughter was using her creativity to object to my call. Rudely, she was texting me a single letter at a time, just as Ashley had shown her. She was determined to interrupt the conversation.

I

H

A

T

E

Y

O

U

.

She said a lot, one letter at a time. I had to smile at her creativity in being obnoxious. All teens have their moments, but she holds the power to make parenting a little more fun. If she really hated me, she would have used an exclamation point. I didn't mimic her back, but I want to point out:

I
L
O
V
E
H
E
R
!

#278. REACHING OUT

I need people
If something is wrong
And I do reach out
To believe me
But also
I need them to
Not scare me
With their response

I need them to
Carry the fire and intensity
To find an answer or solution
A curiosity to listen
And a reminder

That my heart can ask for what

I need

#279. RELEASE

God, I have felt You in pain, now let me feel You in that pain's release.

You enchant me. It is as if You wrap me like a hundred blankets swirling in the arms of a hurricane. I see the wind blow. I see You in the flutter of the leaves. I see Your flirts in the sway of a hammock. The leaves of flowers drum out a proper tune as You play them with Your love.

#280. LEARNING TO BE PLAYFUL

I ask God

Where have You been?

What smells do You bring?

Have You kissed a flower, today?

I smell one on Your breath

As You talk to me

Intoxicating me

With Your love

Stop it, my God

I am serious,

Tell me: how have You filled

Your day?

I finally have time

To settle and feel

But I am still and

Safe

I'm awake

Hey, God

Stop making my head swirl with

That flower's sweet smell

The trash in the kitchen stinks

I think I need flower scented trash bags...

Don't worry, God, I am just playing with You.

#281. A MOTHER'S VALUE

The girls' new counselor has been teaching me. My insights matter. My role matters. I had gotten to the point where I figured people didn't want to hear what I had to bring, so I stopped talking. He's getting me to open up again.

He has been struggling to get my girls to trust him, even though he is humorous, kind, and observant. It's much nicer to feel part of a team than be the one everyone is trying to blame or fix.

#282. GOD'S TOUCH

I taste You in the rain, in the food I eat. I taste the earth. I taste Your inner fortitude that allowed You to break the security of the seed, but I taste something more. I taste You, Your seed, and Your essence. You invigorate my senses, every opening, and every thought.

God, is this how You heal the trauma of abuse? Is this how You get past the shields of pain? Your touch. You touch me in a way more intimate than sex, at least the sex that I have experienced. How do You do that?

#283. ALL IN THE CHEMISTRY

You come
Yourself, not the imprint of Your love
I can feel my body respond
To Your presence
Reaching out
As if I echo back
But it is not
An echo
It's me. My essence calling back

The chemicals in me reach out
Yearning forth
For more of You
You enraptured me

I have a question. Do the chemicals in me fit like puzzle pieces in You? Or are You the puzzle pieces? Is that how neurotransmitters and food flavors work? Is that how You play on my nerves?

#284. SPIRITUAL AND PHYSICAL REALITIES

I finally learned how to switch between being with God and people grace-fully. It made it fun to be able to change as fast as a lamp turns off and on.

#285. HELPING MY GIRLS

I was asked: how should people approach my daughters when they draw-back? I thought about it for a while and then wrote down the only method I'd seen work:

Number 1. Sit with them. If they don't allow that, sit near them where they can see you. Show that you are a safe person. Give them time to trust you.

Number 2. Watch their breathing, their coloring, without making eye contact. Just be aware. Your goal is to be with them and just show that you are non-threatening. Do they have good blood flow to their skin? Are they calm?

Number 3. Follow their lead. Let them mourn, cry, laugh, pull away. Mirror any of their body positions. Engage in their interests. Follow their lead and wait. Let them come to you. Be safe.

Number 4. Share in their interests without trying to teach them any-thing, just be with them where they are. See if you can find any spark of life in their eyes. Any interest, anger, or passion. Your fourth goal is to keep it alive.

If there is ANY spark of interest in life, you are on the right track. Your only goal is to maximize the amount of time it is there.

Number 5. Gradually, you will be able to speak truth into their lives, without losing that spark. That is goal number 5. After that, you can provide resistance, challenges to their ideas and perspectives, if you can keep that spark alive.

At least, that is how my God did it with me and how the one hospital psychiatrist that single-handedly gained my girls' trust in less than ten minutes did it with them. The process can take a few minutes if someone is gifted knowing it, or a few years of trial and error, but it always seemed to work.

I was at a point in which I could answer questions and be helpful, but I felt like something else was going on. I began experiencing God as if He was under water and I had been given magic seaweed to breathe under there. My body ached from the abuse, caring for kids, and the demands of life. Submerging it, figuratively under the veil of the sea, brought it peace, even if I had to occasionally come to the surface to answer some questions.

#286. KISSES

Your kisses reached deep within me and seemed
To tether themselves to my soul
Remember the plan, and the smile You had
A story of love to unfold
A story that's woven with passion and flame
A story that is yet to be told
A story of Krishna with Radha
A story of Christ with His bride
A story that'd marvel even my heart
A story that You shared with pride
So, dear God, I ask You
Your primal delight, Your passion, Your purpose, Your plan
What tricks do You hold? Don't worry. I heard You.

I might be Your biggest fan.

#287. PLAYING MUSIC

Climbing under the sheets, You swim under my skin and skate along my nerves. You fill me and play in me with delight. Is that the energy, the chi, the life? Are You just restoring me in the depths, tonight? What can I do, in response, for You? Whisper words of love, make You blush? Oh Lord, what could I do for You? I used to be exhausted. I would collapse for the night, but now, I could be awake for a while. I feel shy mentioning it laying here with You. You wouldn't be shy, I know. But... why do You say "shush"?

Just listen to You play?

I feel like a stringed instrument, in the hands of a master. Being strummed and caressed. Most people, You know, would have had to masturbate to get this much pleasure. But, God, You are truly able to play the human body. Can I tell You a thought? You should teach Your ways to more men. Being able to do that, holy fuck. There would NEVER be women out on the town at night if You did that.

#288. RAPTURE

Is this how You plan for the rapture? Like a God making love? Like a sign on a parents' room, out for the night? You bind up the fraying ends of my nerves. You settle their never-ending pleas. You silence their pain and free them to feel again.

Did You secretly sneak me an entheogen?

#289. HEALING

My God. If I knew You could heal abuse, a soul that was ruptured like mine, like this, I would have lain my body by Your feet long ago.

#290. WEIRDNESS

God, some people say they hear words when they talk to You. That's weird. Maybe I don't hear words because I listen in pictures. How many languages do You speak? I want to learn some of Your linguist-ease. But don't talk to me in words, that is just weird.

#291. UNDER THE SILENCE

If I were a pot
I'd want to be filled
With the freshest water
Just to let
The wind
Splash some on You

If I were a rock
Filled with minerals
I'd sparkle and shine so that
I could flirt with Your eyes

Some people are sad when they see me
A woman deserted, abused

But there is a truth that they do not know
I share my days, my nights, with You

#292. QUESTIONS FROM ABUSE

What would I have asked You during the years of abuse? If I went back to that room where I was dissociatively dreaming of hikes by the falls? I would ask You what my body was saying. What were the things that were too much for me to hear? A lot of those comments it spoke are still buried.

What does my body say to You? If You put Your ear on it to listen?

Not like the stethoscope of a doctor, just listening to my heart beat, but the ability to listen to the flow and catch of each nerve. The smoothness or catch of a vein. The flow of electrolytes in and out of the cells as they retire from the day.

#293. HIS VOICE

Did You hear the man who raped me? Could You hear the drum beat of my blood as he hit me? Could You listen to the ache of my spirit as he blistered my skin? Are those cells still even there? What did the bruises look like from the inside? What sound did my kidney screech when it was too weak from the stress?

I can still hear the sounds in my head. My blood seems to carry his voice through my soul. God, can You make it stop now.

Why is it that I can start a question and have You answer it so quickly? Not that everything is over or that the trauma and memories have dissolved away, but You are slowly pressing against the memories. You answer my questions and settle them before I even get to the end of them, so there is no question left to mark.

I think I know the difference between God and religion. Spirituality makes challenging topics more palatable. You make difficult situations more manageable; religion just adds on more things to do. I have enough to do without having to pray and repent compulsively.

#294. SHARING

God, do You want to explore Your world with my body? The things You have made are so beautiful, but I can only imagine that part of the pleasure is getting to interact with it. Do You get to do that? Or do You just have to observe passively? What perspective do You view them from? Just watching, but not getting to feel how it interacts inside? Or do You get to feel ALL OF IT? Does each ripple, all over the world, of every energy for every sense, get to move in You? Can You give me a dream of that tonight?

#295. EARTHQUAKES

People always say that the rain is Your tears. Is an earthquake Your orgasm? Just asking.

#296. QUESTION ABOUT PORNOGRAPHY

God, I am sitting here wondering
You see everything that happens on Earth
You could measure the cubic centimeters of oxygen I breathe
In a day

So, since You see everything,
You have watched every single filming of pornography
Right? I mean, if You hear every heart cry with every single pain
And You see everything
Maybe You don't buy it, but Your job as God means
You watched while it was filmed

Therefore, I have a question
People having sex, do they know how to do that innately?
But I have a deeper question
I have never seen anything, from people making love in a movie
To full-on pornography
With people enjoying themselves
It always just looks like they are performing
Is that because they are just performing?

If it doesn't exist, we need some Buddhist pornography
I probably just offended someone, (sorry)
But it should exist
Kind of like martial art movies I like, but naked
That would be too funny
But it might help people, getting them to
Think about
Enjoying their bodies
Being at peace

We need more people who know
Capture enjoyment, not scenes
Not rule books or guilt-inducing religious legislation

But books about enjoying and having fun
With these bodies You made

You did a good job
If I do say so myself
It's a shame, sex and
Spirituality have never seemed
As far apart
As they do in our culture

#297. CIRCLE DANCE

Sometimes
When I think of my life
I feel like I'm at the end
Of a circle dance
Exhausted, enthralled
Dizzy from spinning
In excitement
Longing for one more round
To reach You again

This time
I don't want to wait
For You to dance
With ALL humanity
Seriously, Man
Is it too much
To play a slow song?

I'd audaciously ask You
To dance

And I'd whisper in Your ear
Let's take this round off
My children are all
Cared for content
It would be forward
But, God

Seriously?
I have to admit
We have danced this
Way too many times

All I can say
Thank You for creating the dance
And leaving me
At the end
Secretly resting
Counting the days
Til You could escape
For a night

Is that a plan?
I'll wait right here
You know the address, correct?
Backwards speaking
TijihbA (just skip it, God and I have code words)

#298. NOISE OF CALM

Becca is playing the guitar. The laundry machine is running. Ashley is watching a movie and giggling. Christy is silent working on a Minecraft video. Elsie is in her room lip sinking videos. My home is so much quieter than last year. They all have their interests, friends, and are settling in with their new ways to relax.

It makes me remember a note that was posted in our home years ago. It read, "No mommy aloud." I took those words to heart; be quiet when times of conflict occur with children. If Becca had written it correctly, "allowed," my autistic brain would not have figured it out. I am grateful that my girls have mentored me as a parent, just as I have mentored them.

Don't worry, I have since learned it is "lip syncing," which makes more sense. Ashley encouraged me:

"Their/our. Know rules about grammar."

Sometimes the way everyone thinks is perfect, doesn't make sense. Rules exist for our pleasure and ease, but we still get to master when and how they are applied. Writing is correct when it resonates with hearts, not when every word is spelled perfectly and all the punctuation is corrected to standard convention.

#299. GOD'S EMBRACE

God, I long for Your embrace. But as I hear Your song, every note commands the cells of my body in remembrance. I taste Your sweetness seep into my veins like tea leaves invigorate water.

Your power dares enter even my spit and causes me to drink Your divinity for hours. I can taste Your secret treasures. Do people realize it's real? You were God in human form before. Do You long for that touch once more?

#300. FLIRTING

God, I've come to the conclusion that I cannot flirt. Which is funny when I consider how much I do it with You. I blush at even the sound of Your name.

Oh, does this ever end? Is the real reason we die to pull us out of this constant tension of sex? Like a dirt nap after a REALLY LONG day?

#301. GOD'S HEART

The desert doesn't need rain; it's a desert.

God, I heard Your voice today. Not like people say,
When they hear You speak to them as they pray
I heard Your voice in the heart of a healer
Or maybe I heard Your heart, in his voice,
I don't know
It's so convoluted
As it jumps into my mind

But it touched the same You
That walked me through the memories
The same You
That caught me as I stopped
Breathing

From being hit
It was odd, to be honest
To hear You in a person

He had Your passion
To see my daughters well
He shared Your acceptance
To listen to the details
Of my life and not
Recoil
He's giving his life
To heal

Bless him
God?
There are very few people I would ask
For You to bless the work
Of their hands
But his heart
It shares Your voice

#302. RESTORING MYSELF

The best exercise for me
Is still
Breath and sleep

As the counselors have worked to stabilize my children, I have found that I
have more time just to be. I sway in the hammock and consider all that has

changed in my life over the years. I love to look at the flowers growing in the garden and feel the wind brush across me.

#303. TIME OUT(SIDE)

I'm here today
Sitting in front of the door
With it locked
Three kids inside
I sit with the fourth
Waiting

Patient and
Waiting

For her to calm down
And
Be safe
Together we wait
In time
Out
Side

#304. THE GAME

You are like the childhood game of phone
Telling Your message
Of hope

Through a thousand generations
Only for me to turn
And have You say, "I am here"

I could stick my tongue down Your throat
For such a game
Or kick You in the shin
Hell, I'd have played footsie
With You, the whole time, if I had known

"You tricked me," I'd say
"But, playfully?"
It's true. You'll always win
I love You

Is there another game You have planned?

#305. SITTING WITH GOD

I have learned that there is nothing I can say that God has not heard before. He lets me speak to Him freely, no matter what I am feeling. I play with Him, talk to Him, and sometimes we just sit together.

I wonder if God keeps some of my prayers on His answering machine, saved to listen to again and again, just like I keep some people's messages, because I love their voice. I left Him a message today.

How do You measure temperature? If You took mine would it change? I just wonder, considering thermodynamics, would temperature exist separate from time? We humans measure all sorts of things, but just ignore the reality of time. What we measure as heat is just movement, but without time, would movement exist? Come on, answer, please.

What would my temperature be? Do You have enough insight to know the fluctuations that accompany creation? Is that why women's temperatures change throughout our cycles? You are quiet tonight. Do I have to pose a harder question for You when my first one stumped You? Our intimacy is too much, so I'll conclude:

> God upon god
> Taste me
> I'm sweet like fruit
> Hold on
> Do flavors depend on time?
> After all, it takes time
> To travel the nerves
> Is that how You do it?
> You touch everything
> Without the delay
> You are intriguing
> Fascinating
> No, that isn't right
> You're You
> But You are mine
> Too

#306. A HALLOWEEN MASK

It's silly, but sometimes I try to talk to God in a way that might fool Him of who is speaking. Praying with different accents, I guess. It adds some spark to play with Him that way. Like a kid with a mask, fooling a parent; He will always know.

#307. IN THE FLOWERS

To be honest, I think I see Your face in the flowers.
Your regalness, Your pride. Your bowed heart.
I see Your independence and multifacetedness
If that is even a word
Everything cries out: You

It's like a great artist that signed every work
You made me, too. Can You see You in me?
Am I like a mirror, shining back?
Oh, I hope so
You give me so much pleasure
I'd love to give You some, too

Do You see me as a flower?
What part of You do I play?
What song do You hear in me?

My dad always told me if I made a mistake, make it into a flower. This world full of humans must make You a pretty bouquet.

#308. PEOPLE

I don't get people

When I have a problem
I want it resolved
Not extended in time
With sympathy
Doing nothing
It's just kind
(of annoying)
And (not)
Helpful

I know people try
To force
Comfort
But in my mind
It's just clingy
I'd much rather hear
I don't know
And move on

God, thank You for not being
Like people

#309. PERPLEXED

Frantic people
Are odd to me
They don't even
Know to be quiet

Attention doesn't help
Find what they are missing
The skills needed for
Self-governing
Instead
They choose chaos

How should I respond
If they have not found
In their whole lifetime
A solution

How should I
In 10 minutes
Discover a plan
To set up a coup
And bring peace

Frantic people
Are a mystery
For someone else to solve

#310. MAYBE A FAVOR

God, You are so thoughtful and resourceful. Could You help me be able to share the peace You have given to me? Without words. Please just let me be like the flower or bird sharing Your beauty. I am not sure how You will do it, but there are so many people who don't know how to hear You in

speaking peace. If it has a language, please use me to sing Your song, quietly.

#311. MORE QUESTIONS FROM ME

God, I have an interesting question
Have You experienced sex?
Have You been able to meet someone like You?
Someone who can love You as You are?
Someone who has the power to join with Your essence and
Create something
New?

Are the Earth and the galaxies like that for You?
Sometimes, I wonder
As I look upon all of creation
If You were a teenager—
Wildly casting sperm all over the world
All the trees. All the animals
All the amazing parts of creation

#312. MISSING OUT?

An object itself is only half the fun
The real fun is what it does inside
The chemicals released
The cascades they trigger
Who knows, experiencing them in the rhythm of time

Might be part of what makes them special

All the sensations
Movements of blood
A ray of light
Hitting a rod in an eye
A wave of sound knocking upon
A thin little membrane
A drum
Amazing really
This world You made

But I have to wonder
If You're missing out
On that part
I'd be more than honored
To let You try
If You wanted to see it and feel it
Through me
You haven't existed entirely
If You never felt it first hand
God, You know I am in love with You, right?

People are weird, but I think I have Your number down.

#313. LOOK UP

Our culture fills itself
With demands

Ways to fit in

Have a firm shake

Make contact

With eyes

It doesn't seem

Polite

Eyes tell so much about a person. They reveal hesitancy. They speak out doubt, even when the person's words do not. It feels like reading someone's diary. It burns.

But society has a way of intruding. Butting in. So I try, but all I see is so much. I wonder, God, how can I make eye contact with You? I use my whole body. Can You try to help me do that when I look at people?

#314. NO HEADING AT ALL

Christy threw a chair at her counselor today. I think she still needs to work on speaking. Nothing like striking a nerve with a freaked-out kid. I heard her crying herself to sleep. She likes him; she just got scared.

#315. IN A PERFECT WORLD

Ashley told me that, at school, she was taught, "The best way to end it if you are being chased is to stop running."

Not very wise if the one chasing is set on causing you harm. A lot of advice is written for a perfect world without abuse.

#316. A PASSWORD

During the preregistration for surgery, I inquired, "can I put a password on my account? To ensure I am the only one who can access my information? I have them in place for my utilities."

"We already have safeguards for that," was the reply.

"Really? Like the last four digits of my social security number? My birthday date and place? My mother's maiden name? That's not enough. Those are only effective if the caller is not someone with whom I have shared a bank account, filed taxes, and lived with for years. For access to my account, please allow me to require a password."

Even places that serve thousands of abuse victims a year don't seem to realize the vulnerability of a person leaving a violent marriage.

#317. WHAT'S LACKING

Someone needs to start a service
That scours the Internet
Able to white out details
Of people leaving abuse
Maybe design a program
That abuse shelters could run
There are confidential addresses
And mailing services
But the dangers today
Are embedded online

#318. A SOUP'S SEASONING

God, I stop to eat lunch and decide, You're like a bowl of soup. The subtle flavors seep into the water, creating a broth.

Aw, shit, flashbacks. Really? But You know the timing and the order of healing. I'll trust You (AGAIN), but I still HATE IT.

> Swallow, he shouted
> Love me
> The plea of my heart,
> Just let me go
> "I can't," You said
> "Your life is not over"
> I can't swallow that truth

O, God, if I can taste You in the subtlest change in a broth, You mix flavors with such delight. The herbs each adding their touch. They work together to create complexity, a mingledness, unity. But with him, I tasted bitterness, rejection, fear. A mingledness of pain. For as much as I would like to hate him, to write him off completely, I cannot deny the pain I tasted in his sperm. Was that with You, too? Do You taste our souls like that? Do You taste our broken hopes? Do You like my flavor? Am I filled with pain, rejection, and fear? Despite all that, can You still taste me?

Or is it like this broth? If I just ate bay leaves, alone or with salt, I'd feel sick. The combination of time and a little warmth bring out their life.

#319. POTENCY

Even a drop of You can start a tree.

#320. IMPROVEMENTS

Not including a mandatory kindness mode on humans, that was a mistake. God, it could have at least been an option. You could have designed life like Minecraft, with creative and survival modes. Some of us would do well with those options.

While I am at it, if You are taking notes, You need to inspire someone to create vibrators that play songs with varying rhythms. Variety is believed to be the spice of life.

#321. EMBRACE

God, thank You for holding on to me, as I hold on to them. Sometimes, the world just hurts.

#322. JIU JITSU

I swear Jiu Jitsu is the best teacher for parenting my kids.

> Roll with the punches
> Stay as relaxed as I can, and roll
> Until there is an opportunity
> To take your opponent

I say that, but Elsie takes great pride in being able to flip me over and pin me to the ground.

#323. ALL IN THE ACT

Ashley was stressed out tonight. I could almost feel her wanting to numb out with food, so I tried a preemptive blow. I walked into the kitchen and announced, "I am upset, so I am going to eat this entire box of crackers. And then I am going to eat a few sandwiches." My stomach hurt for hours, but it kept her from binging. She finally saw the ridiculousness of her response. If one night of indigestion for me can lead her from a lifetime of pain, it was worth it.

#324. WHY

What would it take for a man to relax and be content to receive? Then I could sense You beneath the pain and know what to do. Why don't You enrapture them as You do me?

Can I tell You a secret? A quiet, intimate secret? Nope. I am too shy.

You enter my skin and delight me with Your charms.

I would have been killed, hundreds of years ago, for saying such -HERESY-But it is true.

I'll tell You something You know.

"You were my safety, my net from pain."

Little did he know. He couldn't control where You stood.

#325. MY SECRET CRUSH

I went to the mailbox today and felt You.

How is it that a breeze

Can sneak up my sleeve and

Make me blush?

You blew air on my arm, and I felt

Like a woman

Experiencing

Well... the caress of a lover

You touch me even

With Your breath

God, how do You know how to disarm me?

How do You know how gently to touch?

How do You heal a woman who has seen, and felt, and heard all I have?

You get past my defense. A mere breeze under my covering. It's like a whisper from a crush.

God, I like You and our relationship. Not a day goes by that You do not whisper to me.

#326. HONESTY

Can I be honest with You now God? I don't think that my issues are with sex. Their roots seem to be entangled with Frank's use of control and domination. You have taught me, slowly, how to trust my body. How to feel, taste, and inhabit my skin. You've taught me how to rest inside and how to be intimate.

Does domination come from dominion like God's area of command? That seems so odd since You don't lead or command with control, but that is what dominate means in our language. You are a much better leader and lover.

You can make love with my taste buds with orange juice. You can play my nerves like a music box with just vibrations of air from a bird. You can enter my skin, using lotion as Your vehicle. You can play with my eyes using just the wick of a candle, traversing the open space, to create the sensation of touch.

#327. IN RETURN

> God, let each of my breaths calmly stoke
> The flames of Your heart.
> When the coals burn low and
> Your face seems dim
> May my words, and even my silent air,
> Rekindle Your love

People have teased me that God's passion for us never fluctuates. They know of nothing that could change His love, but they haven't heard my story. It can cool even the heart of God and I am certain that there are others with stories like mine.

I still think of You, how You could blow the wind up the corner of my sleeve and remind me of Your touch. Your kisses leave their mark.

#328. EVEN BREATHING

Even when I breathe, I draw You into me and can feel Your presence in the air. I breathe. Oh God, I love You. You are in the sweetness. God, how can even breathing bring so much pleasure? Am I dead? How can You be so tangible? I'd reach out to touch You, but I see You and hear You in my cells.

#329. POLITICS AND DEMANDS

There was a candidate today
Who said that even women
Who were raped
And got pregnant
Should not be allowed abortions
Can I tell you the truth?
Looking at a child
Who mimics your rapist
Smelling their skin
Seeing them move in
Ways that are similar
Can be terrifying
You must give up every part
Of yourself
To do it, to set yourself aside
To raise them
Not just like a typical parent
In those moments when

Your innermost being screams

RUN, you have to be able

To check yourself

Reach out your heart and say

COME, let me be safety

For you

I think it is too much to ask

Someone who doesn't

Know You

#330. COERCION

I officially hate

Elections

I was listening to the debates

And some of the

Candidates

Reminded me of him

They had this way of using

Their cadence and inflection to

Manipulate

Luring people to agree

With them more than

Their ideas warranted

It wasn't charisma, it was

Purposeful manipulation

Of affection. He didn't do it with me

With me, he was just mean
And vindictive, but I heard him
Doing it with others

#331. STRAIN

There are still times that I feel like I am breathing Jell-O; it can be hard to gather the strength just to breathe. God, at points, everything seems to go gray, and my oxygen levels drop. The alligator clip keeps going between the 70 and 90. I know I should go to the doctor, but I don't want to ever again. I feel too confused to drive.

Tomorrow will be better, right? I try to gift myself time to rest.

I am in time out
Not You
If You join me
Here
Be quiet
Be calm

#332. MY ROOM

This is my bedroom
Sacred ground and
Special place
My brother painted
The walls

There is no
Fighting
Here

If you would like
To be present
And feel God's
Grace
To dream
Enter my door
With wisdom

Without a trace
Of loud words
Or insults
Or shame
Or despair
Come and meet
Stillness
In humor
And peace

And
Let Him draw
A smile
Upon your face

#333. STILLNESS

God, do I pull You away from all that You need to do? Like Radha and Krishna, or is more like Jesus with Mary? There are many stories people think of as we to try to understand You, but You encourage me to rest and just be with You.

I don't always get the tasks done around my house as I would like. The years have worn me down. Sometimes I am just too tired. Can You just sit here with me, that is if You are not busy with blocking bullets or working on a President's heart?

#334. THANKFULNESS

I have discovered that there can be something positive and a skill that can be refined or developed even in the most challenging of situations. Even situations that seem hopeless can provide an acceptance of my frailty or death.

#335. ENJOYMENT

> You enjoy my toes with dew upon the grass
> You have let me be like a woman
> With a thousand lovers
> Each drop of water, a friend

#336. BROTHERS AND SISTERS

As I meet each new person
I think
God
You made even more amazing
Delightful, refreshing
People
Even though we may not share the
Exact same DNA
We are brothers and sisters

When my parents adopted
The first time
I wrote a poem
I'll share it with You
But I think of it not
Just with my sisters
But everyone I meet

Every time I think I know
A little more about You
You bring a person along
To show me more of what You created
What You are like

#337. IN THE FRAY

There never was enough
Material for God to share
All the love He had
When He thought
He might have finished
He remembered one more
He wanted to meet
And so the cloth
Of humanity ripped
But with it, the edges frayed
A single strand waivered
Not sure to which side
It belonged
Neither one any better
But both left undone
Finally, it sat
And gave the half stitch away

Was it better to be
The one done first
Rejoicing in being bigger than life
Then learning to give
The half stitch away to cover
Your sister or brother
What is the value of a ½ stitch
Anyway?

A half stitch has no purpose
Alone, ever

When I look at you
One of my siblings
I know our DNA might be
Different enough for others
To question
Are they sisters
But the truth
We were twins once
Ripped from a single
Piece of cloth
Both created by God
As He tried to stretch even just one
More "Another"

#338. CANCER

When we moved, my new doctor looked at my extreme pulse swings as a sign of disease and was baffled by my low oxygen. He did not ignore the symptoms. He did not blame them on PTSD. He did not assume that my heart raced as a sign of anxiety. Instead, he found cancer. I required surgery and radiation. The symptoms were the same as they were before we moved, but I had a new doctor. He saw my body with fresh eyes. If he had known the history of abuse, he may have brushed the symptoms aside and misappropriated them as stemming from trauma.

The diagnosis was hard for my girls, but they weathered it just fine. My parents came and helped, as did my brother. However, it was not until the doctors figured out how to treat the muscle weakness that I could keep up my oxygen levels to make it harder to grow tumors. Regular cells like oxygen, who knew?

#339. PROGRESS

This morning, Elsie got frantic, losing her homework for school. But instead of crying and freaking, she said to herself:

"Ok, stop. Before I lose it, I need to calm down. That way I can find it." I know they don't sound like a kid's words, but they were. She had insightfully scripted her personal intervention to use instead of panic. I am proud of her.

#340. LONGBOARDING

Christy asked me to go skateboarding with her. Me, an unbalanced, poorly coordinated mom on a skateboard. We had fun, and she promised to delete all the videos she took of me as I attempted to join her. I have met people with autism who are great at sports; I have never been one of them.

I am glad that Christy accepts me as I am. There are some things that we can't change, but it always feels good to be included.

#341. A SINGLE AFTERNOON

I came home today to find Ashley curled up on the couch, stoically trying to keep it together. One of her friends is attempting to break up with her boyfriend. Her reason: he was pressuring her to have sex and he hit her.

I got Ashley in the car and started to drive. My first instinct was to get her separated from her sisters, so she didn't bring up issues for her sisters as well. I had driven about three miles when I realized that the five-pm traffic was cluttering the roads. I could feel my body as I started to panic. My brain felt like I had been sniffing glue or getting gas for a car at station with poor air circulation. I could feel myself getting dizzy and nauseous. My hands felt numb. In a moment of clarity, I pulled off in a grocery store parking lot and called my mother.

"Mom, do you have a minute to talk?" That is our secret code for drop whatever the hell you are doing, because I seriously need you.

I told her about what was going on with Ashley's friend. I told her that Ashley felt partially responsible because she had a gut feeling before the girl had even started dating the boy. I thought my mom might be able to relate. I knew she had felt that way with Frank.

I went into the store and left Ashley in the car, on the phone, with my mom. As I shopped, I tried to center myself.

Just one aisle at a time
Blue labels
Blue labels are super reduced
Just look, blue
Breathe
Slow

Ashley is safe
It's okay
My mom has her
I just need to calm
Myself

Abuse fucking sucks

Just breathe
In and out
Try spelling something
I see cheese

C-H- oh my God
E-E- I can't
S-E Shhh
One breath at a time
One pause at a time

I got back to the car. Ashley was laughing, and my mom was telling her about how the trauma she had experienced is part of what makes her compassionate and sensitive. She talked about how PTSD could become a gift instead of a hindrance. It warmed my heart as I loaded the car. I had purchased 16 boxes of the same cereal. Guess I was practicing repetitive breathing on that aisle. Fortunately, they were 98 cents each.

I am so thankful to have my mom as part of our lives.

#342. AND MY DAD

The girls have had difficulty calling God "Father God." They unanimously decided, they would call Him "Poppa God" instead. I think that is the biggest compliment anyone could ever get.

Both my father and my mother embody God's love, gentleness, and generosity.

#343. WHAT I'D SAY

What would I say to all the people who have walked with my family?
Hmm.

The biggest thing
I would share
We made it through the hardest parts
Together, you did your job

Some of you were great
Some of you seriously needed a break
Others of you were just jerks, but
Your colleagues carried us through
So "Good job"
Remember that and keep learning
We are all jerks sometimes
But there is not a day that goes by
That I can look at one of my girls
Without bowing my heart
In appreciation for you
And the passion you had
To work tirelessly
To let us experience
Life another day

#344. REGARDLESS, IT WORKED

I have always thought it was stupid that people talked about finding a needle in a haystack. I figured just get a magnet or burn the whole thing down if you don't have a magnet. Whatever the method, you all got the job done.

#345. NOT AUTISTIC

Some people say I don't seem autistic. It's kind of funny to me, but I lived for years without telling anyone and coming up with all sorts of strategies. They say I don't look autistic. They don't think I sound autistic, well at least before they read a book like this. Even then, some people contend that I can play with words and tempo too much to be autistic.

I have had to learn how to see something from another person's perspective, grasp the meaning of words that sound the same but look different, and understand pacing. I did not even want to do all the typesetting for this book, but Ashley informed me that everyone does not like large print books and normal people do not slow down if the text is justified (blocky) and the words are more separated on one line to the next.

As I chose the order of the poems and stories, I have tried to capture the cadence of life after trauma. Somethings whiz by, flashbacks impose themselves, surprises happen. The real question people need to consider is not if I look or sound autistic. They need to ask if autism affects how I think and live? It takes time to discover that answer. It takes patience.

The same logic can be applied to trauma. People sometimes comment that I do not look or sound like a person with PTSD. Appearance and words are things that often change first, but trauma is great at wearing disguises. It silently walks around; it acts out its role as denial with the power to numb or alarm. More important than if I look and sound like a victim of trauma is does trauma affect how I think and live.

Trauma can hang out in a life for years masquerading as a friend. Healing can be slow and take years of self-reflection, triggering events and challenges, and love to rip off trauma's masks.

#346. HUMOR

Family support is not just about coming to watch kids or sending money for school supplies even though those things are helpful. Family support is also being able to laugh and cry together.

This year, my annual mammogram was concerning and I needed to have additional screenings to rule out breast cancer. When I went back for the second mammogram, the doctor decided I also needed an ultrasound. In the end, it turned out I just had lots of cysts and some fibroids; I did not have cancer again. The next day, after all the procedures, I went to see my brother. He's conclusion from the saga was that I had earned a new nickname.

"What 'Cysts'? Like 'Sis'?"

"No, Crunchy Tits."

One has to love a family with a sense of humor. But on a deeper level, his wisdom and approach to life have guided me through many obstacles. The way he looked at things and his approach to difficulty and problems have mentored me. I am sure he lives unaware of his impact and blessing.

The best way I can describe it: my brother is a master weaver. I see him making a beautiful braid, masterfully weaving denial, humor, and reality together. Rhythmically, pulling it in, making it manageable, an impressive result. By itself, denial would leave one ineffective and distant. By itself, humor would just seem misplaced. And, while most people would argue that reality is the best thing to acknowledge, sometimes it is too much without the lightening effect of humor and the ability to grace oneself with denial on occasion. So I look at my life and try to apply what I've learned from him; switch between the three. Whenever there is too much of one, just weave in a few more strands, until all the reality, all the humor, and all the denial are pulled together in a beautiful tapestry.

#347. ENCOURAGING WORDS

I have many letters from my mother. One card reads, "We love you so much. I know that your life is much more complex and difficult than you could have anticipated. I know you will prevail because you are smart, strong, and supported by your friends, your church, your belief in God, and us- your family." Another reminds me to be bamboo and not oak; bamboo can bend and sway when the wind and storms hit. It does not religiously hold its position and refuse to sway.

#348. DAY DREAMING

There is no value in holding anger toward Frank; I have learned reflection and wisdom can keep me safer than judgment. I hope he has moved on and has learned the errors of his ways. For the sake of his new wife, I pray he can genuinely laugh and think of others. But honestly, narcissism can be deadly. Very few people overcome it. And for me, it is a different day.

When the stories do come up, I take them to God. His touch is more than enough to tickle my life. Sometimes I ask Him why it all happened. Was Frank just grumpy? Self-centered? Did he ever feel shame? I ask God, too, if He ever felt shame.

#349. GOD, ARE YOU STILL LEARNING

How did You know how to touch me to heal and yet not teach Frank so he didn't abuse me in the first place? Are You still learning? Did You mess up the first time and have to learn a new way? I attempt to reassure Him, "It's okay, I do that, too, sometimes. Don't worry."

I give God a hard time when I can. I tease Him by saying that service dogs are reincarnated Buddhist monks. After all, they must be attentive, alert, restrained, and willing to serve. Plus, they eat and are grateful for whatever is provided while they work tirelessly to ease suffering.

My relationship with God has held many different emotions. Like all strong things, it has been tempered over time and purified by intensity.

I've been trying to help Christy trust me that she can have thoughts of suicide and yet rely on all the people around her to help her get through them. It's taking a while for her antidepressant to kick in. I would have never guessed that being able to outlast thoughts of suicide would be a skill to develop, but it is. I hope we are successful and can make a difference before she gets overwhelmed or gives up.

#350. LOSING A CHILD

I have had some friends who lost their children to suicide. One woman lost her daughter. The girl battled bipolar depression before she killed herself. We met a few years after her daughter's death. As I shared some of my struggles, she confided in me that she never blamed her daughter for giving up. She told me that most people do not view mental illnesses as diseases that can be fatal. Her wisdom has helped me appreciate each day I have with my girls.

My daughter today
Keeps talking of death
She startles when
A teacher yells at the class
She demands
Safety and time
Over and over
Wearing me out
But is it that really
Any different
Than a boy struggling
With cancer

That child's parent
Is worn out, too
Staring at life
Unsure what to do
Hoping for life
But aware
Of death's power

It makes me look
At my daughter
Aware
She has a disease
That can be fatal
Her words and reactions
Inside

Battling
Emotional tumors
Invisible to others

I'm not sure
She will win
But I know I do not
Want to waste
Even this moment
Judging her cries
Not seeing her response
As the boy that
Vomits up chemo

Depression
Like cancer
Can be fatal

I try to remember the woman's wisdom, when one of my girls is panicking or triggered. I can work with them to fight, but depression can be fatal; may I never take for granted how long we'll have.

It is hard to be grateful for days and weeks of struggles. It is hard to look at life and realize this is not the last day of the fight.

#351. IF ONLY A DAY

My friend lost her daughter today. She lost her son a few years ago. The grief, I don't know how she will make it through.

Please let her truth rock me as it begs my spirit to feel her pain. Let time heal her sorrow no matter how challenging life becomes. In the midst of hell, help both of us value the life that remains.

#352. CHRISTY STILL STRUGGLES

One of Christy's friends tried to commit suicide. For weeks, Christy fought her own thoughts of ending her life. I tried so hard to help her.

I tried to teach her to trust what God had shown me. She could have whatever reaction she needed, and she could trust the people in her life to help her stay safe. She could experience all her anger and grief. There were ways to feel those emotions without hurting herself or others. There were people around her to help her face all of grief and shame without becoming lost in it or needing to die.

#353. LEAVING

People comment that they will be going to Heaven when they die, but part of me wonders, why did God create all this just to have us escape and be in Heaven? It is kind of like the logic of suicide, the great escape. He worked hard on this Earth, and it is amazing. Is Heaven like his do-over with improvements?

> I must admit
> I like it here
> Sure, there is pain
> But I get to play
> With water in the sink

As I do the dishes
I get to feel the wind touching
My face as I walk to the park
Able to see colors, with all their variants
Painted on a petal of a flower
To experience change
In temperature
As I walk across a room

God, is this how Buddhist monks
And nuns
And gurus
And saints
Can be celibate
You secretly teach them to play
Through their skin
On Earth

#354. SEX AND AWARENESS

What would happen
If we combined
Awareness and sex
Do You know
Without a body
How could You
Find out

Do You wonder?

How did You create something
For humans
If You never experienced it
As a person?

Or did You secretly experience it
ALL
And You just didn't tell anyone
You are so not like
Guys in this culture

#355. MY RESPONSE

I hear people tell their children, "You're getting on my nerves," but I think that is a rollercoaster ride that only God can take.

#356. TRAUMA BOND

People do not always understand the impact of abuse on individuals in a family when they experienced it together.

I beg you
Realize the complexity
Of a trauma bond
Realize the effects
Of dissociative flashbacks
Confusing reality

Realize that transitioning to trust
Another person
Requires believing
Everyone else
Is safe

There is so much to realize
Realize it is too much

#357. SAFE PEOPLE

One of the hardest things I have had to teach my kids is that community workers are safe. The police help people. Doctors try to figure out what is wrong and want to make people feel better. When children are not used to feeling safe as children in a home, it can be hard for them to feel safe anywhere.

#358. THE WALL

Rebecca covered an entire wall in her room with quotes and drawings that inspire her. I wonder if her soul is plastered with them as well. It is amazing to see her embracing life and finding a passion for healing.

#359. VALENTINE'S DAY WISH

I know some people sit and pout
Wanting chocolates
Or kisses

Or time

But this Valentine's Day wish

It is mine

May You touch people

Who dedicate their lives

In service

To speak in ways

That are healing

So that others can

Feel kindness

People want to help

But they just do not know how

Show them

Provide insight to see

Words they can speak

Their service

Is so desperately needed

#360. MY HOPE

Imagine my child

Someday

When you know how

To make peace with yourself

And how to be safe

You can tell them what you felt

What could have worked better

for you in that state
I bet they will listen
When you are not as upset
And your words then will carry
Their burden, their weight

Someday will be coming
You'll make it I know
I'll keep that hope growing
Just trust me, you'll know
For I have a secret
A treasure, a bow
I've fashioned an arrow
And God, well
He bent
Graced it with perfection
And lest they relent

Aim, my dear child
And grace you will claim
The power and strength
Of the truth
Of your name

Don't worry about
The names that they call you
For deep in my heart
I know for a fact
That they'll meet How

You, in your power
Set right and content
With beauty, not hidden
Found How, never sent
A message
You'll teach them
And with that, they will meet
The man I call "How"

Then they'll know
To address you
With words that are kind
From a heart that is gentle
And a, finally, pure mind

#361. MY PRAYER

God, please be like a cupid, connecting hearts between the healers and those that are sick.

#362. CELEBRATION

We celebrated Rebecca's one year anniversary of not cutting. Honestly, I am amazed that she has been able to do that. Not because of not cutting, but the skills and ways of viewing the world that she has had to develop to accomplish that goal. Choosing friends that are peaceful and kind. She sends out recovery message texts every morning. Just something short to help others and keep herself focused on recovering.

#363. DRIVING

I've heard people talk about having God in the driver's seat of their lives and giving Him the reins. Doesn't anybody want to have their dad teach them how to drive?

#364. ENOUGH

Elsie told me she gets enough correction from her sisters. She just needs me to be encouraging and comforting. Thank God she can explain to me what I can do to fulfill that request.

People say that kids should come with manuals. I think they do. Parents simply need to be patient as their children develop the vocabulary to read it to them. Plus, parents need discipline to focus their attention, and nurture their desire, to listen.

#365. SWEARING AND DISGRACE

I don't think single words exist in our language to justly honor the pain and disgrace of abuse. As my daughters mature, I imagine they will learn to wield metaphors and imagery instead of overused cursing. But insight and discrimination must be earned over time with effort and practice.

#366. NEWS

Another man killed his wife. I hate the news. It takes me back to that moment, reminds me that even now he could find us. Cover me, God. Cover us. Be like a shadow that keeps us safe.

I go to bed and weep. Becca finds me. "It's okay, Mom; he can't find us here. It's okay. Mom, you got us here. We're safe now. Remember, we did it. We're all right."

Elsie walks in. "Mom is just having a hard time. It's okay." She walks out unaffected. They're growing up. They are making it.

Becca now mentors people online. Thousands have signed up to read what she writes about life after trauma.

#367. NATURAL RESPONSE

I saw a post online that talked about visual patterns and anxiety. It was about poisonous animals and the patterns on them causing people to feel uncomfortable—raised heart rates, fear, agitation, need to reconcile things. I looked at the patterns and just found them fascinating. I wasn't scared. But then again, I have wondered if that is part of what helps most people learn to read faces.

#368. DEPTH

I read a caption today. "Believe her. Her description of the violence is only the tip of the iceburg."

#369. LAUGHING

When the girls have friends over, they laugh so much! I love to hear their excitement, loud and humorous. I still don't follow what they are finding funny. Sometimes I think they laugh just because it feels fun to wiggle like that.

#370. MOODINESS

Even when they get moody or are talking back, I am glad my daughters are responding to the world and learning to think for themselves.

#371. CIRCULATION

Can You ride on a single cell of blood? As if it were an innertube in a flume? Can You inhabit me in that way? Can You see, feel, and hear what I sound like from that perspective? Can You be omnipresent and yet still pull all Your attention to that small of a place? Have my body be the world for You, like this world is to me? I want to ride on Your Spirit like that and hear the journal of events riding Your pulse, with Your heart marking the elapsement of time.

#372. NEEDS

My kids have many needs:
To be left alone to relax
To have friends visit and talk
To engage with books
To play sports
To have space and time to discover
Who they will be and
What they will need

#373. THOSE WHO HURT

There is wisdom in not being hurt by the words of the hurting, whether children or strangers.

#374. FRUSTRATION AND PRIDE

It is easy to be inconvenienced, impatient, and rude while waiting in need. I try to ask myself when someone is slow and distracted, can I see beyond my frustration and pride? Can I see where they may be stuck?

#375. OUR BEST

Each generation
We try to do better
We try to pull all
Of the lessons we've learned
Together
Hence, it would follow that
Each person
I speak to
Is a product of time
And effort
Dozens of generations
Refining approach
Sharpening insight
Trying
If I stand here

Impatient and
Rude
I will miss
This masterpiece
That dozens
Have worked
To create

Each person embodies
The wisdom
Of centuries
Of work
The only task left
Get along

I am certain
I've annoyed people
Wasting their time
And I am grateful
That they subdued
Their self-serving plea
To silence
To be there in that moment
Imperfect
Alongside me

#376. A SMILE

I met a woman who uses the same words as Frank did when she prays, but the smile on her face is the same one I have when I am with You. Her face, it's an expression I know so deeply in my soul, it blocks out her words so that I can't even hear them. She is beautiful when she prays.

#377. CALMING IT DOWN

When my kids start yelling
Or throwing insults
I tell them
I am deaf to your words
They are stealing your power
To share
What you are trying to say
Could you try again
But this time
Change the approach
So it is not too
Distracting

Powerful words
Get their strength
Not by volume or shock
But with their unwritten
Invitation to share
Our experience, our life

With the strength

To communicate

Feelings

And perspective

Powerful words dare

Use the air

To touch

Hearts

Those are the words

That help me

To hear

Can you try

As I learn to listen

Again

#378. PLAYFUL THOUGHT

Playing with air is one way that time, space, and insight all interact. It's a concept that probably doesn't make sense to a lot of people, but I will try to explain.

People play in the air

Their extremities forming angles

Their movements defined

By time

Each person draws

In breaths

And they hold them
Waiting, refining
The air
Sharing
Exchanging
Exhaling
Speed as they
Speak

I watch people and observe how they move. Do they pause before or after their breath? Do they have a catch in the flow, impeding their breath, or are they slow? How do they mediate between speaking and breathing?

The variations
Seem endless

I prefer to see how people capture ideas and what they let be instead of listening only to their vocabulary. People are fascinating to study and watch.

#379. WAIT

I just realized my idea and speech in high school about a mandatory dress code with neon separates might not have been well received. That may seem completely random, but I am enjoying being able to have random thoughts pop up that have nothing to do with trauma.

#380. PLAY THERAPY

Someone asked Christy what she does after I tell her she has done too much Minecraft, but I don't ever say that to her. It's play therapy for kids. Create a world, be violent, don't get things right. It's all okay in online-land.

#381. QUOTE OF MY LIFE

I saw something that made me laugh so much yesterday. It said, "Leave me alone. I have been awesome all day and need to do it again tomorrow." It is true.

#382. NEW SKILLS

I found a new way to look at having to teach the girls the same skill time after time in different ways.

> They do it again and again and again and again
> And every time from the first through the last, I reply
> The same
> "Thank you for yet another opportunity to teach you"
> Hopefully, someday, you will have corrected my teaching
> Until I have get it
> Gotten it
> Right?

#383. EVERYONE IS SPECIAL

There is a way to undermine isolation
Multiply the value of those who surround you

It is easy to feel alone
At times, even fun, to revel with self-pity
But there are too many people
Alone in this world
The grocery clerk
The banker
A gasoline clerk
Alone, really

If you truly listen
You'll find
There are plenty of people
Who need
Someone with time
And perspective
To listen

Listen not to their
Prewritten scripts, what they say
But to their true passions
Their insights
Challenge yourself
To connect with something

Deeper than
The surface dug out by
Shallow words that are spoken

Are they
Okay?
Is something off or distinct
In their well-rehearsed speech
Is there
A catch in their voice
Undertones of emotions
Subtle cues frequently
Missed

Everyone is special
With insights
To find
Hurts to be softened
In need of your time

Just be peaceful
And open
To their state
Each day
Listening softly

It is hard to
Feel lonely
When you listen like that

#384. LEARN TO LISTEN

It is a skill to be receptive, supportive
Content to be kind

#385. MINISTRY

Just being quiet is a ministry in a loud broken world.

#386. PET PEEVES

It bugs me when I see people correcting their children:
Do this. Do that.
You don't do it right.
Clean your room.
Stop talking back.
Nagging and commanding taking turns as if they were steps in a dance.

What about the skills of:
Learning to pace oneself
Being a person of character with the ability
to evaluate what to do oneself
Being able to persevere and move on
in the face of failure?

Tirades and criticism do not teach children.
They illuminate the parent's issues.

What kids can learn from them:

How to be demanding

Inflexible

And how to feel perpetually inadequate.

For kids overcoming trauma, I think this is even truer.

#387. I DON'T GET IT

People ask, "How do you talk to God? How often do you pray?" as if it is a discipline you can not do. You can't NOT talk to God. He speaks a lot of languages, even silence. Where do people come up with questions like that?

God, are they trying to ask, "How do You listen?"

#388. EXISTING

My girls asked me how I know God exists.

"Because I exist," I replied, "you can't make something this amazing by chance."

"Couldn't you just know you exist because I exist?" one questioned.

"No," I answered, "because you exist, I know I have limits and boundaries. I know that we both get to share this amazing experience together."

#389. A PIECE OF ADVICE

Never think you know the end of your story. God is the author of life, and He loves a good mystery as much as He loves each of us.

#390. SPORTS CAMP

Christy and Elsie spent a week at sports camp. The police department hosted the program. When Christy came home, I asked her what she learned at camp.

"I learned bald people can be safe." Her dad was bald.

She can now go to the grocery store and ride in the car without panicking if she sees a bald man. All I can say, her group leader, "Officer Baldy," did more in a week by being calm and kind than a few years of therapy had done.

Just a reminder, officers, you make a difference even if you never know how the littlest things have changed people's lives.

#391. I HATE YOU

Christy walked in the door today and announced, "I HATE YOU." She was hot, stressed, and tired. It would have been easy to reply, "You can't talk to me like that; go to your room; you're grounded."

But if you step back and look at the situation another way, she was like a baby not sure how to get help. Body sensations like heat, discomfort, and pain force my child to feel her body. It would be hard to be so uncomfortable, and struggle, ignorant of how to regulate the sensations.

Why should I criticize or punish her, when she is letting out what we all just bottle up and repress? She is like an infant, tired, hot, and hungry, but now she has words. "I hate you" is harsh, but it states the same thing as a baby screaming in pain.

I decide to look at her as a baby. "I'm sorry. You must feel awful. It is hot, and you are probably tired and angry." I ignore her words, hearing them instead as a cry, "I need you and am in discomfort and I don't know what to do, and I need you to help me, but you haven't helped me yet. Therefore, I am mad."

Instead of offense or punishment or anger, I offer her an idea, a thought. "One thing that helps me when I am too hot, and I feel overwhelmed by my day, is a refreshing bath. It limits sensations and sounds as I cool off. It might even help cool off your emotions. I could draw you one if you want. You could wear a swimsuit and pretend you are swimming.

An hour later, she is snuggled beside me, on the couch, asleep. She let me wash her hair as she cried. She apologized for saying she hated me. She remembered how to relax.

The secret was learning to see where she was developmentally. There are hurdles from her early youth. Things that she didn't learn in the confusion, including how to be soothed when in pain and learning to trust that pain won't last forever.

She is still learning how to be present in her body, how to overcome the flood of unpleasant sensations and express her need for comfort and help. She may need a better script, but she was just saying what we all were thinking: it is too damn hot and I don't like it, and I am pissed that I haven't been able to figure out how to make the sensation stop.

The way I look at it, my job as a parent is not about controlling her behavior. Instead, she is better served by me guiding her as she discovers methods that will work for her AND others.

#392. CONFLICT

Elsie is currently learning how to be angry and express herself adequately in conflicts. I secretly hope she doesn't need an all-out verbal fight. It is so hard for me to keep a straight face and be incessant when, internally, I am proud of her for staying present and showing up to defend her stance.

#393. LABELING

In our society, people think of emotions as good or bad. While it is true that certain emotions are easier for parents to contain, when dished out by their children, I think there is a fundamental error in categorizing emotions this way. Our feelings, all of them, can be helpful if we recognize them correctly and respond to them with insight.

If one of my daughters comments, "I am bored," I want her to be able to decipher why. Is she bored because she has outgrown her old interests and needs to try something new? Is she bored because she is neglecting something she needs to do and needs to get back on track? Does she need to spend some time with friends or go for a walk, because she is feeling isolated or lethargic and is confusing that feeling with boredom? To find out the answer, she must practice the art of reflecting her inner desires.

#394. EMOTIONS

Each of us needs
The security
To investigate and learn
Why we feel the way we do

To be strong independent
Of the reasons behind
Our emotions

Each one can be felt
More important is
The emotion's intent

We control the expression
Directing our path
With skills learned by others
Who knew how to lead
Hearts
And feelings

Calming
Settling
Restraining
Refraining
Encouraging
Building
Strengthening
A person's natural bent

Knowing when
To draw an emotion
Closer
For reflection
Limiting the impact
Mitigating the pain
Of pity or strife

And when to share

A secret, corroding a soul

For healing

They know even when

To set their own

Emotions

Aside

To enter in

The response of others

Honoring the trust

And connection

Carefully discerning

How to use our response

To help others

Manage emotions

With us

#395. THE VALUE OF OUR FEELINGS

We all need to have the skills to maximize our emotions, to restrain them, and to feel them. Each emotion contains immeasurable potential if an individual knows how to honor its expression and power.

#396. DISCIPLINE

I don't think people know what they are talking about when they speak on the topic of discipline. They confuse discipline with punishment.

Discipline to me is all the things you do to keep yourself strong and on the right path. Disciplining my kids is teaching them how to regulate themselves so they can handle crises.

Discipline is eating consistently. It is avoiding gossip and drama. It is building relationships and maintaining friendships. It's making sure people are getting enough sleep and clothed appropriately for the weather. It's teaching them better ways to speak and interact with themselves, and others, so that they can be content, functioning women. Beating them or yelling at them wouldn't do that. It might make them quiet, but it doesn't discipline them.

#397. THE TURKEY

I dropped dinner on the floor tonight. A whole, fully-cooked turkey. The dog thought he had been promoted to King. I was a bit pissed at myself. Christy called me to sit by her. She told me, "Mom, let me hold you. It will be okay. No one is mad at you. Here, I got you." She rubbed my back and gave me a hug. God, thanks for letting her hear that in the recesses of her soul so strongly that she can echo those words back to me. Dropping the turkey was a small price to pay to hear her say that.

#398. FIELDTRIP

I went on a field trip with Elsie's school today. We went to a skating rink. I think I parent more like a dad than a mom. That might be weird to say, but it's true. I am direct, don't get involved in drama, offer practical solutions, and am firm on consequences. I guess I get to be both in a way. Now that I think about it, it's a lot like my mom's approach.

#399. CAPACITY

All of us are connected
In a giant world circuit
As we live on this Earth
United and touching
Feeling the charge of
Each person
As we bristle along
Together

God, do You feel all of us
Through the connection
Or do you feel each of us
As separates

We try to control
The flow with rules
Social demands
Religion
Laws
Desperately attempting
To smooth out our flow
Be effective
Prevent the shock
Of anger and selfish desires

But, despite all our effort

There is still pain
There is still abuse
Of power
There is still selfishness
And greed
Worry
There will not be enough
Power

We turn on the news
Hear the repulsive
Inhumane acts
Killing and rapes
Daring to stand up
To You
Able to defy
All our measures
Spitting in the face
Of You, God

But the worst part
There are many cries
Still muffled by walls
Held in silence
In homes
That hours of video
Or reports
Could never contain

Occasionally
One seeps through
And begs
Screaming its truth
The words of a friend
Or the face of a neighbor
Reveal horror
Help me honor
The courage

Embolden my eyes
To carry compassion
And teach my heart
To respond
I know You are the God
That created this world
Help me find the response
That fits

I'm certain You
Would love
To enforce
Gentleness and kindness
Reigning as kings
Within every home

But I wonder
If You could do all that
Wouldn't You

I am pressed to believe
You do what You can
Transforming hearts
Respecting our lives
Doing everything
To mentor us
Teaching us
To bring relief to
The hurting
Like You

But if the cries can be heard
By my ears
The ones You created
A little violence
Has spilled over
What You can handle on Your own

So please
Let me listen and answer
Those cries that I hear
Grant me that capacity
Meeting demand
Splitting the current
Until
The intensity is buffered
The amplitude mitigated
The charge evened out

Help us, God
Maybe together we can
End it

#400. ANCESTORS

Sometimes I imagine sitting with my ancestors plotting and planning how to overcome the trauma of generational abuse. What could we do to solve the puzzle? What would we need? In the dream, I volunteer to walk through it. No one ever thought someone would be crazy enough to volunteer for that. It's just a dream, but it helps me feel more in control of my experience.

I feel like I can hear them apologize and say, "We've never had someone crazy enough (nor autistic enough) to take us literally and try it!"

#401. MOVING ON

There have been a lot of people who have helped bring stability to my family. It has been an honor to watch people walk alongside us as we've healed. Every time that someone moves on, I smile. Whatever lesson that they needed to learn from us, and whatever lesson we were to learn from them, is done. I always pray for them to be blessed as they are promoted to their next endeavors.

Lately, I have wondered if death will be like that, too. When I contemplate the impact of my time here on Earth, I wrestle with the question of if I will finish my purpose in time. It's good. It makes me write, but it is still

a question. Will my life, and the way that I have lived it, make a difference?

I don't know. I have to look at books of facial expressions to even de-
code my interactions each day. There are so many things that take me
more time; yet, I can do other things that a lot of people cannot do at all. I
hope that my weaknesses do not silence my life.

#402. PROGRESS

The counselor that saw all four girls moved on with his life. All the girls,
except Christy, have graduated to seeing counselors in an office and not at
home.

Christy's new counselor was a bit disappointed. She had helped Christy
make progress, but then the girl regressed. I encouraged her. It's still progress if either one of you is alert and able to change. When my child re-
gresses, she is simply saying, "I didn't quite figure this out the first time."

Even if all that happens is the adult being able to be innovative and discerning and changing to a different approach, progress is being made. It's
only when no one can change that development lay stagnant.

#403. CHOICES

I took Becca to the store. She asked for raspberries. She said it was because
they are sweet and taste like candy and she knew I would buy them without my "Candy may only cost a $1, but there is an invisible dental debit
card charge of $130" speech.

Elsie had a migraine today. She looked at me and said, "I am going to
comfort myself by taking a cold salt bath." It sounds SO SCRIPTED, but

that is what you get when an autistic mom and a dozen counselors parent a child.

#404. CHANGE

I sometimes wonder if my life experience has changed me. I think back to my earliest memories with autism. I reflect on being at girl scout camp and having a friend tell me that if I wanted to wake her up at night, to pour a glass of water on her head. I did. We are still friends to this day.

I wonder if this experience has taught me how to feel and how to react. But, more importantly, I pray that the story of my family will somehow be used to encourage, convict, enlighten, challenge, and touch others. Maybe through this book it will.

Violence, and violence in families, shatters souls. It destroys people's hopes, dreams, will to live, and ability to recover. But trauma, whether from childhood, dating, marriage, or war, can be mended. It just takes time and enough people working together.

#405. PROJECT OF RESTORATION

There are things I could not fix. I could not fix our home where we lived when the kids were small. I could not even go back to that city for years. But instead of selling it, my brother took it over. He fixed it. He replaced counters and sinks. He fished out crackers from the heating vents that I had missed. He painted, knocked out walls, and refinished the floors.

Years after we left, I finally felt strong enough to go back. It was a relief to see all that my brother had done. He had taken a house, worn out by abuse, and turned it into a home finished with grace. The 8x10 bedroom that had housed two bunk beds, or one with two cribs, looked so small without furniture. The marks on the ceiling were covered with paint.

If it were not for meeting my brother, I would have never gone back. He is special. For whatever reason, just being around him relaxes me.

#406. STORYTELLING

Looking back at my story, I am reminded to see it through my own eyes. I was literal when I said that I see white shapes left on the page and not letters encoding each thought and phrase.

> God, this is my final request
> For each person
> In need of the space
> And the words
> To wrestle
> Life's hurts to the page
>
> Grant them
> All that they need
> Peel up my letters and lines
> And spin them together
>
> Then create
> A magical thread
> Leave the circles as beads
> And weave me
> The cover that my life
> Lost as I wrote

My story, my pain

And there on the page
Just leave white
With plenty of room
For each reader to write

Free the pages
Each written
So there's plenty of room
And this book gets so worn
That a half-stitch remains
And then
Breathe anew

But, God, please safeguard
The dear binding
Until it's healed
Every heart
Then finally
With peace
Let it
Depart

#407. THE END

With love and grace,
Sophia

Included Poems, Prayers, and Narrations

#1. TYING THE KNOT.. 1

#2. REALITY SINKS IN 2

#3. THREADING THE NEEDLE 5

#4. ASKING WHY 6

#5. SWEARING 7

#6. BABY FACTORY 8

#7. SCARED 9

#8. NEEDING HELP 9

#9. HOW AM I DOING 10

#10. THE ANGRY CRY OF PAIN 11

#11. APPLYING FOR FOOD STAMPS 12

#12. SAFEGUARDS.. 14

#13. WIC OFFICE 14

#14. THE PEDIATRICIAN 16

#15. THE ONE TO BLAME 17

#16. NEEDING SILENCE 18

#17. THE WEAVING 19

#18. DEFEAT 19

#19. PLEADING FOR REST 19

#20. TAPESTRY OF MOONLIGHT 20

#21. CONTRAST 22

#22. LOOKING GOOD... 22

Sophia Grace

#23. SELF-CARE 23

#24. THE NARRATIONS OF LIFE 24

#25. A DROP 26

#26. WEAKNESS 26

#27. MISUNDERSTOOD 27

#28. INTERVENTION 29

#29. THE ILLUSION 30

#30. DISAPPOINTMENT 33

#31. IMPENDING ISOLATION 34

#32. ONE NIGHT A WEEK 35

#33. CHILD WELFARE 36

#34. THE QUILT 37

#35. POLICE 39

#36. ON MY OWN 40

#37. SIMPLE SOLUTIONS 40

#38. RECOVERING 41

#39. POSTPARTUM DEPRESSION 41

#40. INTELLIGENCE 42

#41. ASKING FOR PEACE 42

#42. A SPLIT-SECOND BREATH 43

#43. PROBLEMS 44

#44. MORE OF GOD 45

#45. RESPITE 45

#46. ADVICE 46

#47. A PENNY A PAGE 46

After the Violence

#48. FLOUR 46

#49. THREAT LEVEL 47

#50. STOP EVERYTHING 47

#51. PARADIGM 48

#52. THE CHEERIOS 49

#53. UNFAIR 49

#54. THE OCEAN 50

#55. LOSS 51

#56. THE LOCKSMITH 51

#57. BUCKLING 52

#58. PINNACLE OF PAIN 52

#59. ASKING FOR HELP 53

#60. MAKING THE MOST OF AN AWFUL SITUATION 54

#61. WHY NOT JUST TAKE A PILL 55

#62. DEFENSE 58

#63. ANTICIPATION 60

#64. THE VEIL OF NORMALCY RIPPED 60

#65. DOMESTIC VIOLENCE AND SEX OFFENDER TREATMENT 60

#66. BOUNDARIES 61

#67. REINCARNATION 61

#68. REVENGE 62

#69. NAÏVE 63

#70. THE BOND 63

#71. BUT WHY DOESN'T SHE GET IT AND LEAVE 66

#72. ESCAPES 66

#73. TRUST 66

#74. FAMILIES 67

#75. IT'S JUST CAUSE AND EFFECT 68

#76. TRAUMA BRAIN... 72

#77. WORN OUT 74

#78. TERROR... 76

#79. START OF A NEW YEAR 77

#80. MEMORY 78

#81. RECOIL FROM PAIN.. 78

#82. DESPERATION... 79

#83. LIFE NEVER STOPS 79

#84. LITTLE THINGS.. 80

#85. GLITTER... 80

#86. PNEUMONIA... 82

#87. ALARM.. 82

#88. DIVORCE 84

#89. THE PULL TO REMEMBER 84

#90. CLINGING 85

#91. ENDURANCE.. 86

#92. LA LECHE 86

#93. MENTORING.. 87

#94. PERSONALITIES.. 87

#95. VOCALIZING OUR TRUTH.. 88

#96. ONE DARK NIGHT... 89

#97. A CROWN 91

After the Violence

#98. LETTING GO 91

#99. CONSIDERING DEATH 91

#100. HICCUPS 92

#101. TIME 92

#102. FEARS 93

#103. GOING BACK TO SCHOOL 94

#104. TOO SLEEPY TO FUNCTION 94

#105. BODIES SPEAK 96

#106. HOLDING A FRANTIC KID 97

#107. THE BRUISES 98

#108. THE ATIVAN 98

#109. WEEKENDS 99

#110. HOME 101

#111. 'TIL MORNING 101

#112. SUNRISE 102

#113. LIKE A POP-UP CARD 102

#114. NARCOLEPSY 103

#115. SOCIOPATHS 105

#116. DETERMINATION 106

#117. A MOMMA"S LOVE 106

#118. RULES IN THE SANDBOX 106

#119. THE POWER OF PRAYER 110

#120. PRUDENESS 111

#121. AGGRESSION 113

#122. WEAKNESSES 114

#123. ANGER 114

#124. UNCLEAR 115

#125. NO WORDS 117

#126. THE BENEFITS OF SCHOOL 119

#127. BEGGING GOD FOR A NEW CHALLENGE 119

#128. DOCTORS TRY SO HARD 120

#129. TURNOVER 120

#130. IMAGES 122

#131. STORIES 122

#132. MY REQUEST 123

#133. APOLOGY 124

#134. A MANTRA 124

#135. CALMING DOWN 125

#136. NOMINATED 125

#137. SELECTED 126

#138. PLAYING ONLINE 127

#139. PRONE TO INFECTION 128

#140. CHANGING THE TRAJECTORY 131

#141. CHILD DEVELOPMENT 132

#142. WRONGLY DIVIDED 135

#143. TOTALLY CONFUSED 137

#144. NOTE TO SELF 138

#145. UNAVAILABLE 140

#146. FRANK'S NEW GIRLFRIENDS 142

#147. DISTRACTION 142

After the Violence

#148. REGRET..143

#149. LITTLE THINGS..143

#150. WITHOUT AN ANSWER 144

#151. BROKEN...144

#152. INSIGHT...145

#153. REDIRECT 145

#154. SHAKEY 146

#155. PERSISTENCE...146

#156. WEAK 147

#157. NURTURING CHILDHOOD.......................................148

#158. A DREAM 148

#159. FOLLOWED BY ANOTHER DREAM 149

#160. TUCKED IN WITH A STORY.....................................151

#161. BEDMATES...152

#162. PRESSURE...152

#163. FRIENDLY ADVICE 152

#164. TEARS 154

#165. HEALING..155

#166. FINDING COMFORT..156

#167. SOCIOPATHS ON TV..156

#168. A SOCIOPATH'S TELLS 158

#169. RECIPROCITY...158

#170. PHONE VOICE..159

#171. UNCERTAINTY..160

#172. WISDOM..160

#173. FOR HEAVEN'S SAKE..161

#174. CHILDREN'S PAIN..161

#175. EARPHONES..162

#176. TO DO LIST...162

#177. A SCHOLARSHIP..163

#178. MAKING ROOM..166

#179. UNIQUE..167

#180. A DOSE OF HUMOR..168

#181. IMPULSIVITY...169

#182. DOCTORS, UGHHH...170

#183. ELSIE..172

#184. HOW TO RESPOND...172

#185. FIGHTING FIRE..173

#186. STANDARD FOR SEX OFFENDERS...174

#187. GUILT..175

#188. MY PART...175

#189. PORN...176

#190. BALANCING...177

#191. SUPPORT..177

#192. MY RESPONSE...178

#193. A WEEKEND EACH MONTH..179

#194. SUPERVISED VISITS..179

#195. MANIPULATION..180

#196. STAIRS...180

#197. DOWN HILL..180

After the Violence

#198. ALONE 181

#199. BINGING OR STARVING 181

#200. DINNER 183

#201. WHITE NOISE MACHINE 183

#202. PARENTING 184

#203. STRAIN 184

#204. COURT 185

#205. ESCALATION 185

#206. WHAT HAPPENED NEXT 186

#207. LOST AT SCHOOL 186

#208. BUT FOR CHRISTY 186

#209. WORDS TO CALM 188

#210. SPLIT IN TWO 188

#211. CHRISTMAS SITTERS ARE HARD TO FIND 191

#212. FIGHTING 194

#213. RECONNECTING 194

#214. CHRISTY'S NEEDS 194

#215. LYING ALONE 194

#216. SOLUTION 196

#217. ANOREXIC 197

#218. RECOVERING 197

#219. ATTENTION 198

#220. FISHING 199

#221. SERVICES 199

#222. NAME CHANGE 199

#223. EVEN THIS 200

#224. CLUES OF ABUSE 200

#225. LETTERS 201

#226. INQUIRY 201

#227. DISCONNECT 202

#228. ABUSE INVESTIGATION 202

#229. JAPANESE CRANES 203

#230. BODIES SPEAK 203

#231. APPROACH 204

#232. VISITORS 205

#233. INTERPLAY 205

#234. GROWING 206

#235. REVOLUTION 207

#236. THE SKY 207

#237. INNOCENCE 208

#238. THE ER SOCIAL WORKER 209

#239. STUPID 209

#240. GRADUAL CHANGE 210

#241. ME 210

#242. CONTENT 210

#243. A THOUSAND IDEAS 211

#244. NEXT 212

#245. WORDS 213

#246. GOD'S PAIN 214

#247. UP A TREE WITHOUT A LADDER 214

After the Violence

#248. JUST GIVE ME LESS 216

#249. RESIDENTIAL TREATMENT 216

#250. MY CHILDREN 218

#251. MY BODY SPEAKS, TOO 219

#252. HELPING THE GRIEVING 221

#253. EXPECTATIONS 224

#254. MOVING 225

#255. THE NIGHT THAT SEALED IT 225

#256. SUICIDE AND THE CREST OF COURAGE 227

#257. ANY WAY POSSIBLE 229

#258. CHRISTY AND A ROAD 230

#259. INTERSTATE 231

#260. REALISTICALLY 232

#261. BUGS 232

#262. RUNAWAY 232

#263. THANK YOU 234

#264. TO THE OFFICERS 235

#265. UNTRAINED WORDS 235

#266. HUMAN TELEGRAM FOR A DAY 237

#267. MY SHOES 237

#268. THANK YOU 239

#269. QUIET AS SLIPPERS 240

#270. HENNA 241

#271. TEASING GOD 241

#272. A THANK YOU LETTER 241

#273. NEEDS... 242

#274. JUST A THOUGHT 242

#275. GOD THINKS OF EVERYTHING 242

#276. EVENING WALK 243

#277. PHONE WARS 243

#278. REACHING OUT 244

#279. RELEASE 245

#280. LEARNING TO BE PLAYFUL 245

#281. A MOTHER'S VALUE 246

#282. GOD'S TOUCH 246

#283. ALL IN THE CHEMISTRY 247

#284. SPIRITUAL AND PHYSICAL REALITIES 248

#285. HELPING MY GIRLS 248

#286. KISSES 249

#287. PLAYING MUSIC... 250

#288. RAPTURE.. 250

#289. HEALING 251

#290. WEIRDNESS.. 251

#291. UNDER THE SILENCE.. 251

#292. QUESTIONS FROM ABUSE... 252

#293. HIS VOICE 252

#294. SHARING 253

#295. EARTHQUAKES.. 253

#296. QUESTION ABOUT PORNOGRAPHY 253

#297. CIRCLE DANCE... 255

After the Violence

#298. NOISE OF CALM 257

#299. GOD'S EMBRACE 257

#300. FLIRTING 258

#301. GOD'S HEART 258

#302. RESTORING MYSELF 259

#303. TIME OUT(SIDE) 260

#304. THE GAME 260

#305. SITTING WITH GOD 261

#306. A HALLOWEEN MASK 262

#307. IN THE FLOWERS 263

#308. PEOPLE 263

#309. PERPLEXED 264

#310. MAYBE A FAVOR 265

#311. MORE QUESTIONS FROM ME 266

#312. MISSING OUT? 266

#313. LOOK UP 267

#314. NO HEADING AT ALL 268

#315. IN A PERFECT WORLD 268

#316. A PASSWORD 269

#317. WHAT'S LACKING 269

#318. A SOUP'S SEASONING 270

#319. POTENCY 271

#320. IMPROVEMENTS 271

#321. EMBRACE 271

#322. JIU JITSU 271

#323. ALL IN THE ACT...272

#324. WHY...272

#325. MY SECRET CRUSH...273

#326. HONESTY..273

#327. IN RETURN...274

#328. EVEN BREATHING..275

#329. POLITICS AND DEMANDS...275

#330. COERCION..276

#331. STRAIN...277

#332. MY ROOM...277

#333. STILLNESS...279

#334. THANKFULNESS..279

#335. ENJOYMENT...279

#336. BROTHERS AND SISTERS..280

#337. IN THE FRAY..281

#338. CANCER...282

#339. PROGRESS..283

#340. LONGBOARDING..283

#341. A SINGLE AFTERNOON...283

#342. AND MY DAD..285

#343. WHAT I'D SAY..286

#344. REGARDLESS, IT WORKED...287

#345. NOT AUTISTIC..287

#346. HUMOR...288

#347. ENCOURAGING WORDS..289

After the Violence

#348. DAY DREAMING 289

#349. GOD, ARE YOU STILL LEARNING 290

#350. LOSING A CHILD 290

#351. IF ONLY A DAY 292

#352. CHRISTY STILL STRUGGLES 293

#353. LEAVING 293

#354. SEX AND AWARENESS 294

#355. MY RESPONSE 295

#356. TRAUMA BOND 295

#357. SAFE PEOPLE 296

#358. THE WALL 296

#359. VALENTINE'S DAY WISH 296

#360. MY HOPE 297

#361. MY PRAYER 299

#362. CELEBRATION 299

#363. DRIVING 300

#364. ENOUGH 300

#365. SWEARING AND DISGRACE 300

#366. NEWS 300

#367. NATURAL RESPONSE 301

#368. DEPTH 301

#369. LAUGHING 301

#370. MOODINESS 302

#371. CIRCULATION 302

#372. NEEDS 302

#373. THOSE WHO HURT 303

#374. FRUSTRATION AND PRIDE 303

#375. OUR BEST 303

#376. A SMILE 305

#377. CALMING IT DOWN 305

#378. PLAYFUL THOUGHT 306

#379. WAIT 307

#380. PLAY THERAPY 308

#381. QUOTE OF MY LIFE 308

#382. NEW SKILLS 308

#383. EVERYONE IS SPECIAL 309

#384. LEARN TO LISTEN 311

#385. MINISTRY 311

#386. PET PEEVES 311

#387. I DON'T GET IT 312

#388. EXISTING 312

#389. A PIECE OF ADVICE 312

#390. SPORTS CAMP 313

#391. I HATE YOU 313

#392. CONFLICT 314

#393. LABELING 315

#394. EMOTIONS 315

#395. THE VALUE OF OUR FEELINGS 317

#396. DISCIPLINE 317

#397. THE TURKEY 318

After the Violence

#398. FIELDTRIP 318

#399. CAPACITY 319

#400. ANCESTORS 323

#401. MOVING ON 323

#402. PROGRESS 324

#403. CHOICES 324

#404. CHANGE 325

#405. PROJECT OF RESTORATION 325

#406. STORYTELLING 326

#407. THE END 327

www.ingramcontent.com/pod-product-compliance
Lightning Source LLC
Chambersburg PA
CBHW030418290526
45786CB00001B/30